Becoming an Exceptional Leader

14 Accomplished Leaders in the Disability Community
Share their Stories of Envisioning and Creating
Amazing Disability-Focused Offerings

If they can do it, you can too!

With foreword by Eileen Grubba

www.MaiLingChan.com

Mai Ling Chan, LLC
Phoenix, AZ

For information, address Mai Ling Chan, LLC at 3219 E Camelback Rd, STE 404, Phoenix, AZ 85018.

·

Cover design by Christie Mayer

Edited by Cori Wamsley

Printed in the United States of America

Mai Ling Chan LLC

ISBN: 978-0-578-73684-6

Acknowledgements

Organizing my first anthology was much more challenging and rewarding than I could have ever imagined. Because the authors were selected from previous podcast episodes, this project took over 20 months and 51 episodes to create.

Getting to the final publishing stage would never have been possible without the endless support of my loving family—my husband, Cameron Svendsen, and my children, Nick, Alex, and Raegan.

Without the gift of genuine curiosity and reverence for people's life stories, this book would not exist. For this, I thank my mom, Rosalba Chan. It is because of you that I lean in so hard and value the moments of true connection.

Being genuine is courageous. I thank all co-authors of this book for trusting me to share your story with the world. Your impact is a never-ending ripple, and I am honored to be a part of your journey and help others be moved by the momentum that you have created.

We are never alone in creating beauty in the world. I'm forever grateful to the people who lead me, stand beside me, and sometimes hold me up: Kan Chan, Matt Chan, Lori DiBlasi, Laura Stevenson, G. Patrick Polli, Thomas McDowell, and Mary Huston.

I am so grateful for the creativity and expertise of the following people who truly helped put this book together: Jennifer Baljko—initial editor, Cori Wamsley—final editor,

Christie Mayer—book cover, Stacy Raske—marketing, and Angela Smith—branding. I truly couldn't have done it without you.

And finally, thank you to each author for your willingness to revisit your journey and trust in me to help share your beautiful message with the world. This book is nothing without YOU.

Table of Contents

Foreword

Eileen Grubba

Actress, writer, producer, and advocate for the inclusion of people with disabilities in film, TV, and advertising

Photo by Kevin Sheffield

Welcome! Mai Ling and I first connected when she invited me to be a guest on her Xceptional Leaders podcast in early 2019. I shared with her audience my personal experience with disability, how it informed me of how much work was needed for humanity to realize the importance of people living with disabilities, and the value they add to our world. We spoke of how my life experience sparked my fire and passion to create a more welcoming society, and then drove me into an industry-changing battle for greater diversity and inclusion in film, television, and marketing.

Through her years of interviewing thought leaders and game changers in the arena of advancement and education for disabled people, Mai Ling encountered incredible stories of accomplishments and breakthroughs that raised the bar for disability inclusion and helped move society forward, improving the quality of life for many in disabled communities. Yet, knowing how far behind our world is in terms of becoming an all-inclusive, fully supportive, equal-opportunity society, Mai Ling decided she needed to do more to help future thought leaders rise up, take their place among the leaders, and help push our world even further toward those goals. So she decided to curate some of the stories that have made a great impact so far. She wanted to learn what inspired these leaders, what drove them to create change, what obstacles they encountered, how they overcame them, and what they learned along the way.

Every author she has invited to be a part of this book has had life experience or family experience that forced them to realize a great need. Their ideas required them to courageously move forward. When they faced immense adversity, doubt, and fear, they somehow found their way through and are now sharing their stories and their wisdom in the hopes of making someone else's journey a little easier.

In my early years of advocacy, I was flying by the seat of my pants, figuring it out as I went along, but every time I encountered someone who had experience with creating change, I drank in their stories, absorbed their wisdom, climbed on their great shoulders, and progressed a little more every day. It would have been so helpful to have a book compiled with so many valuable thought leaders sharing their battle stories!

This book will be important for the disability community as it offers experience, insight, and advice to anyone who is driven to help advance education and quality of life for people living with disabilities. Every generation builds upon the advancements of the creative thinkers and doers who came before them. This book gives readers specific tools to follow their dreams, build on their inspiration, and take action. It also provides hard-earned advice about how to succeed. Every person who makes a sincere effort helps us all move forward, so my hope is that this book will encourage more people to take action now and help us end the inequality and inaccessibility that has too long been the accepted standard of the past. I hope it will help us create a fully inclusive, fully accessible, completely equal-opportunity world for everyone who follows.

I'm very excited to support Mai Ling and her chosen co-authors while they make their mark on our next generations of game changers. Please let us know how it helps you and how you are now changing our world for the better. Life is a game! Play it well. Every single one of us has the power to make a difference. Peace! #ALLin

Eileen Grubba is an award-winning actress and a lifetime member of The Actors Studio and has spent more than 26 years on the stage. She recently appeared in HBO's Watchmen, *CBS's* SWAT *and* All Rise, *NBC's* New Amsterdam, *and Netflix's* The Politician, *and just before this publication, she shot a guest star spot in ABC's* Stumptown. *She has been in many films and TV shows, including NBC's* Game of Silence, Sons of Anarchy, Criminal Minds, Bones, *and* Fear the Walking Dead *and HBO's* Hung & Enlightened, Benched, Instant Mom, CSI: Miami, The Mentalist, Cold Case, Nip/Tuck, The Closer, *and* Monk, *among others. She has been nominated three times for Best Actress awards for Indie films, with multiple wins for Best Ensemble Cast in the female lead. She has also won multiple awards for her disability-inclusive short films and screenplays.*

Eileen was paralyzed from the waist down as a child after a vaccine attacked her spinal cord, leaving her with a C1-C4 injury, and she later beat cancer, likely caused by radiation exposure during her medical battles. Doctors said she would never walk again, but she regained most of her mobility through relentless persistence and many surgeries. She is grateful to members of The Actors Studio for teaching her to use her life challenges in her work.

Eileen is an accomplished actress, writer, public speaker, and producer. She is an advocate for the hiring of people with disabilities in film, television, and advertising, serving on the SAG-AFTRA National PWD Committee, and is a brand ambassador for Global Disability Inclusion. She was selected for the CBS Leadership Pipeline and is now going through the program for directing. A fighter all her life, Eileen refuses to give up her quest to create equal opportunity for people with disabilities, and believes inclusion in entertainment will create a world of greater acceptance for everyone.

My Community

Listen to my episode on the Xceptional Leaders podcast:

Extreme Life Experiences Deepen Acting with Eileen Grubba

Ways to Connect with Me

Instagram: @EileenGrubba

Twitter: @EileenGrubba

Facebook Official Page: https://www.facebook.com/EileenGrubbaOfficialPage/

IMDB: https://www.imdb.com/name/nm0344190/

Introduction

It is impossible to ignore the needs of one billion people globally, who identify as having a disability. "One-fifth of the estimated global total, or between 110 million and 190 million people, experience significant disabilities." Of the 61 million people with disabilities in the United States, one in four Americans are estimated to have disabilities that impact major life activities, and nearly one in seven Americans provide care to those with disabilities.[1]

The Americans with Disabilities Act (ADA), passed in 1990, is a civil rights law prohibiting discrimination based on disabilities. The law's passage came at a time when people with disabilities experienced widespread and systemic discrimination, with little to no support or representation. Children with disabilities were systematically excluded from public schools. Individuals were denied healthcare. Residential treatment facilities were inhumane, and most public buildings and transportation systems were not accessible. These are only a few of the many human rights that were routinely denied.

As Robert L. Burgdorf, Jr., author of the first draft of the Americans with Disabilities Act bill (1988) recalls, "In 1971, a New York judge described people with disabilities as 'the most discriminated [against] minority in our nation.'"[2]

---

[1] "Disability Inclusion." The World Bank. October 2019.
https://www.worldbank.org/en/topic/disability#

Thirty years after the implementation of the ADA, access to jobs, schools, transportation, and healthcare have substantially increased, but much still needs to be addressed. Unfortunately, people with disabilities continue to be one of the most marginalized and excluded groups in society. In addition to the broader education, healthcare, safety, and transportation issues, daily accessibility challenges still reduce overall independence and quality of life.

The question is: Whose responsibility is it to continue to advocate for universal access to all human rights for people with disabilities?

Fortunately, for the world, a growing number of disability-focused leaders feel empowered, committed, and determined to make an impact. They are active at all levels of government service, as well as in the private sector, and serve through nonprofit organizations and trendy technology start-ups. They use all resources, talents, and experiences to support their actions, and they are truly leaders in their communities.

I believe strongly in the power of language and have referred to admirable parents, educators, therapists, caregivers, and thought leaders as "Exceptional Leaders" since our first days of creating our online education platform, XceptionalED. The term "exceptional" is increasingly utilized within the special education community and includes individuals who require more challenging instruction, as well

---

[2] "Why I wrote the Americans with Disabilities Act." The Washington Post blog. July 24, 2015.
https://www.washingtonpost.com/posteverything/wp/2015/07/24/why-the-americans-with-disabilities-act-mattered/

as those who require modifications to access the curriculum. More and more, the term is being used interchangeably with "special needs" and less broadly with "disabled."

Recognizing people as "Exceptional Leaders" clearly defines a unique focus of intentions and accomplishments, and I have been honored to spotlight and share their educational platforms and personal stories. After completing 51 Xceptional Leader Podcast interviews in one year, I knew that I still hadn't done enough to celebrate and share what I had learned from my amazing guests. Although I love the podcast medium and strongly connect with the emotions elicited from hearing a person's voice, I also knew I could reach many more people through digital and physical books.

This book is a beautiful collaboration of stories shared by my Xceptional Leader podcast guests. I have invited these amazing disability leaders to expand on their episodes with a very personal look at their journey, vision, inspiration, challenges, and accomplishments.

In the following chapters, you will meet an amazing woman in Nigeria dedicated to educating and uplifting people with disabilities; a man in England who, after exiting his accessible travel company to join Airbnb, continues to motivate and inspire; and a talented and determined teenager wise beyond her years.

You will also learn about how technology leaders are working toward digital accessibility. For example, you will read about people working with Microsoft to create accessible controllers so more people with disabilities can enjoy playing, developing safe online gaming platforms for neurodivergent individuals and mental health communities, and providing disability support education shared through podcasts and online learning.

The film industry is also represented by international, multi-award-winning film producers spotlighting real-life experiences and challenges.

Parents and advocates of people with autism share their devotion to research, education, community, and long-term goals such as independent living and employment. This includes general skills in addition to highly specific careers such as working in a local coffee shop and in digital animation programming.

Authors connect deeply through bestselling books, uniting parents of children with autism, and teaching children about disabilities through beloved characters and stories.

Although these stories represent only a few of the growing number of disability-focused offerings in the world, they provide universal themes that tie them together.

We are all people who are passionate about dedicating our lives to supporting people with disabilities.

For many of us, writing our chapter has been the first opportunity to stop and think about the journey that has brought us to this present moment. Normally, we are hyper-focused on planning, creating, fundraising, developing, celebrating, and at times, overcoming disappointment, so we haven't really had the opportunity to reflect. Several authors have told me that the writing process was, at times, emotional but, ultimately, valuable to their own understanding and appreciation of their efforts.

It is also important to share the fact that our journey to creating this book occurred immediately prior to and during the spring of 2020, when the World Health Organization (WHO) declared the novel coronavirus (COVID-19) outbreak a global pandemic. The combination and timing of several worrisome events—the coronavirus pandemic, stay-at-home confinement, widespread recession, the high unemployment rate, and the great amount of social unrest in the wake of systemic failures—gave us pause. These events raised many questions, doubts, and concerns about our individual and collective health safety, overall economic well-being, and our beliefs about equality, fairness, and justice. The authors of this book have faced varying degrees of these same issues at different points in their lives. The inner strength, determination, and resourcefulness they have used to overcome personal setbacks, push through societal discrimination, and offer their gifts to the world provide a beacon of hope we can model as we navigate these uncertain times.

As leaders on the front lines of supporting our communities, we were called upon immediately to support, create, organize, research, connect, and balance our own self-care. This severely impacted a few of our writer's abilities to complete their chapters, and unfortunately, completely prohibited one writer from moving forward with the project.

One author requested to include his personal experience during the required "shelter-in-place" period in his chapter. His story is a beautiful representation of an

Exceptional Leader's dedication and commitment to his community during one of the most challenging times in history.

The most important message of this book is our invitation for you to join us.

As Simon Sinek, author of *Start with Why* says, "There are only two ways to influence human behavior: you can manipulate it or you can inspire it."

We invite you to explore an intimate look at the "how" and, more deeply, the "why" behind what we have been working on all these years in the hopes that you will reflect on your own gifts and possibilities.

To inspire and support you, we have also included specific reflections on what we have personally gained from our experiences and our recommendations for success, should you choose to embark on your own disability-focused endeavor. These should be seen as our hard-earned pearls of wisdom from someone with a lived experience. You never know what may be helpful to you someday.

As we revisit the question of who can take on the role of advocating for universal access to all human rights for people with disabilities, we enthusiastically say, "Anyone and everyone!" Anyone and everyone can become an Exceptional Leader. It is our collective wish that after reading our stories, you will be inspired to find ways to increase access to equality for all people with disabilities. We hope our successes, setbacks, goals, and gifts guide your vision—your exceptional idea—for creating a more equal world.

Part I: Putting it Into Words

An Imperfect Journey

Words aren't Everything

Mai Ling Chan

MS, CCC-SLP

Photo by CoHoots

"Why do I do this to myself?" I ask myself this question every time I'm about to speak in public. I must be a narcissist or a glutton for punishment. As I wait for my turn to stand up and start speaking, I can feel the heat surge in my body and the single bead of sweat drip down the front of my chest. *Dang it!* I'm pretty sure it's too late to back out of this presentation.

I look over to my co-presenter who is wrapping up her section. I wonder if she is aware that I struggle with word-finding. Is she curious to see how I make it through my part? As a fellow speech-language pathologist, she must have noticed the times during our casual conversations when I circumlocute around a word, hesitate, stutter, or just say, "What's that word?" to see if she can help me find it. Everybody probably knows. I'm just fooling myself with the notion that it's my "little cognitive secret."

I wasn't a speech-language pathologist when the actual incident occurred that changed my life forever. I was actually just beginning my classes in the master's program at Arizona State University (Tempe, Ariz.). Returning to school ten years after completing my undergraduate degree, I was juggling full-time mom duties with a seven- and four-year-old, along with the stress of studying and achieving as only a Type A personality can do.

I was getting ready in my bathroom early one morning when I suddenly felt a "BOINGGGGG" sensation in my head. My eyesight went blurry, everything started spinning, and my right arm became tingly like when it "falls asleep." Feeling the wall with my left hand, I made it to my bed and lay down. My heart raced as I tried to figure out what was going on. *Should I get to the phone to call 9-1-1? Or, maybe if I just lie here and remain calm everything will be OK.*

That episode occurred 16 years ago, and I have kept it a secret from my family and friends for a million poor reasons. This includes not wanting to worry my parents, being afraid to find out it might be worse than I thought, ruining my "perfect" reputation, and the best one, denial. I'm sharing this with you now because it is an important part of my current story.

I ended up staying in bed the rest of the day and, luckily, all acute symptoms eventually passed. Although I was considerably shaken and slightly worried about how serious the incident actually was, I moved forward gingerly and eventually got back to the business of life.

Now I know what you're thinking: I should have immediately gone to the doctor. That is obvious, in hindsight. But since I was relatively young, naive to the seriousness of the event, and terribly busy at the time, it was much easier to put it behind me and focus on daily tasks. I absolutely acknowledged it as a "sign" that I might be stressed with the demands of graduate school and made a mental note to "slow down"—whatever that meant.

As I continued taking speech and language classes, I learned about cerebrovascular accidents (CVAs) and resulting aphasia (a language disorder). Based on my experience and residual symptoms, I cautiously self-diagnosed. The most likely option was a transient ischemic attack (TIA). TIA is a stroke that typically lasts only a few minutes with a temporary period of symptoms, similar to those of a stroke. This diagnosis has never been medically determined, because it was at least two years before I really understood the gravity of what had happened and just accepted it as a passing event. I was dangerously ignorant and uninformed. I truly believe that my blessing at the time was being in an academic program that required intensive cognitive effort combined with a high level of language-centered activities. I was essentially in "rehab" but didn't realize it.

Additional cognitive issues have fluctuated throughout the years. It's possible that these are unrelated to the event and are more a symptom of my very active mind, but they are present nonetheless. This includes mild short-term memory loss, word-finding issues, and difficulty with focused auditory attention. I am very aware of when I'm having a "bad day," doing mental gymnastics to just get a sentence out with ease. These deficits haven't been overly detrimental to me because, stemming from my professional expertise in cognitive rehabilitation, I am a master of strategies. For example, progressing from written checklists to online software that syncs with my calendar and smartphone, I am able to maintain a highly organized and effective system. Take these tools away, and I don't know what I'm supposed to be doing tomorrow.

One night, I had an experience that finally exposed my secret to my husband. We were on our way home in the dark, and I was driving. By that point I had navigated through our neighborhood for at least two years. I should have been able to talk AND drive. Suddenly, my husband said, "Where are you going?" and all the alarms went off in my head. I made a right turn and, at that moment, I was lost. I blamed it on a combination of things—it was dark, I was tired, we were talking so I was distracted. The truth was I had no idea where I was or why I had made that turn. I quickly figured out that I was only a few blocks away from home, and I was able to correct our course.

That was the beginning of some difficult and honest conversations that have continued for almost six years since the wrong-turn event happened. Since then, he has always been included in my little secret. It is because of his encouragement and support that I even considered tackling a high cognitive load activity like public speaking, and yes, I am now monitored by wonderful physicians for any possible cerebrovascular concerns.

Unfortunately, what really impacts me the most in my daily life are word-finding difficulties—and the universe has a sense of humor! My mom says I came out of the womb talking. I'm a "talker," and love everything about language (*I'm silently correcting your grammar*). When my aunt suggested that I become a speech therapist, I saw how it was the perfect career choice for me. How ironic is it then that a speech-language pathologist, a language expert, struggles with a language disorder?

As I type these words, I feel as if I'm removing the veil and coming out of the "I am perfect" closet. I vacillate between cringing and courageousness. Now everyone will know and recognize the deficits I've been trying to hide for years. Fortunately, I'm finally secure with myself and certain that my current tears that flow after years of fear and hiding will turn to relief when my beautiful family and community embrace me with their unconditional love and support. I know now that I should have trusted and included them sooner.

How does this relate to my journey? Since the BOING event in my bathroom, I earned a master's degree in communication disorders from Arizona State University and have provided clinical services as a speech-language pathologist for 14 years. Working in a wide breadth of areas, I have experience in early intervention through end-of-life, with both educational and medical experience. In all of these settings, I have held space for the person I am working with, waiting patiently as they work through activities, sharing their accomplishments, and acknowledging their frustrations. I have grown so much in my appreciation for the beauty and individuality of all people.

Throughout these years I have had the honor of working beside parents, teachers, therapists, and advocates who devote their lives to supporting people with disabilities. Although I enjoy working directly with children and adults with disabilities, I have always felt compelled to contribute in a larger way.

Over the years, I have focused my experience and skills as a second-generation entrepreneur on creating, supporting, and celebrating the people who are making a difference in the disability community. Since 2008, I have provided and supported independent speech-language pathologists to provide services to school districts and families in Arizona through a small staffing company.

Beginning in 2012, as I merged my love of technology with creative therapy activities, I met fantastic speech-language pathologists who were already embracing the iPad and sharing their expertise with the world through software applications, blog reviews, and presentations. I immersed myself in this new and vibrant community and quickly realized what my true calling was: to support and shine a spotlight on these and other inspiring people so that, together, we could reach and help more people.

Since then, I co-created two online education companies (YappGuru and XceptionalED), providing continuing education to disability professionals and caregivers. To date, we have served more than 30,000 students in more than five countries, and support 55 disability leaders to share their expertise and help more people with disabilities. In addition to my own podcast, Xceptional Leaders, I also support and grow the Xceptional Podcast Network, a family of podcasts dedicated to educating, entertaining, and supporting the disability community.

I admit I have quietly struggled with challenging cognitive issues throughout the years, but I have not allowed it to stop me from creating and living a beautiful, purpose-driven life. While I see public speaking opportunities as blessings, I typically over-prepare and practice to reduce language or recall struggles that will most likely arise.

I have always felt my most important challenges are related to the people I serve. As I mentioned earlier, using accountability software to organize tasks and remind me of my responsibilities has been THE strategy that has allowed me to support, achieve, and grow with the people in my life. I would never have been able to remain accountable and reliable to my teams had it not been for my strengths in organizational strategies and tools. Recognizing these challenges, in addition to creating and utilizing a systematic process of support systems, has been my most valuable gift to the hundreds of parents, teachers, therapists, and advocates whom I have worked with over the years.

In addition, having access to the entrepreneurial journeys of so many accomplished and inspiring people enriches my knowledge and understanding of the growing disability industry. I also share this knowledge and my own expertise, through one-on-one consultations, school district presentations, day workshops, and my "Brilliance Zone" program to help guide, support, and connect future disability-focused leaders.

As you can see, I have not allowed challenges to restrict me from fully embracing my strengths and employing those to their fullest capacity. I have been recently described by Lucas Steuber (Augmentative and Alternative Communication [AAC] expert, renowned linguist, speech-language pathologist, app creator, and three-time Best of Computer Electronics Show winner) as "the highest-energy entrepreneur I've ever met in my life as well as probably the—or at least one of the—most well-connected speech-language pathologists across all domains of our scope of practice (not just AAC)." These are definitely characteristics that I am proud of: highly focused actions while engaging with an amazing community of like-minded people.

Through in-depth conversations and watching progress over the years, I have found the common bond between all disability leaders is not the money-making aspect that our "great idea" has earned for us, but the deep fulfillment that comes from truly and deeply connecting with another person. Call it "heart-centered," "purpose-driven," "a calling," but do not call it "work."

Those of us who have chosen to pour our expertise, passion, finances, and futures into our offerings are "Givers." We give freely of all this and more, with the highest goal of helping a person with a disability. Becoming financially wealthy is often not the driving force behind our vision. Although earning money and staying "in the black" is a necessity and must be achieved, abundance and prosperity come in so many other ways, including the personal stories of triumph and achievement as a direct result of our efforts and the ability to communicate, achieve, dance, play, travel, love . . . the list goes on!

I have been so moved, touched, and inspired by stories of joy and heartbreak, success, and challenge. The most touching of these is hearing the ripple effect that our efforts have in the world. From the effort of one person, so many other people benefit. For example, our family of disability-focused podcasts has reached people all over the world! This means people know more about speech therapy (Speech Science podcast), augmentative and alternative communication (Talking With Tech podcast), how to run a private therapy practice (Private Practice Survival Guide podcast), and the amazing stories of global disability leaders (Xceptional Leaders podcast)!

This ripple effect has helped me heed my calling to share these distinct voices on a podcast and curate these amazing stories into a collective book. It is my greatest honor to work with all of the amazing people on these offerings. I can only hope that my own little ripples continue to grow and support people with disabilities to live a fulfilling and joyful life.

My Gifts

I've been asked several times, "Do you make enough money from all of this?" I used to feel very defensive about this question. What amount of money would make my efforts seem valuable to another person? Did they know how many times I woke up in the middle of the night with an aha moment or another great idea? Did those times cost more than the idea I had during the day? Can I quantify how full my heart is when an XceptionalED presenter has 400 people enjoy and benefit from their Live Webinar? Or how much value can be attached to an email from a student sharing joy and gratefulness for being able to learn remotely from Australia and looking forward to helping people with disabilities there?

I am culturally half Colombian and half Chinese, and consequently, a unique combination of two fun-loving but very hard-working parents. I am honored to say that all that I know about business was learned from their in-the-trenches and human-to-human way of connecting with the world. Their actions were guided by deeply held principles upholding respect and support for all people.

Adding to the gifts of a supportive family, experiences such as ongoing personal development and years of rich human-to-human clinical service have helped shape my view of the world and my place within it. I'm finally living a life that is guided and blessed in so many ways. After many achievements and disappointments over the years, I have realized, accepted, and finally embraced the fact that I am not motivated by money. I am 100% motivated by truly deep and meaningful connections with people, the accomplishment of purposeful work, and being genuine. These bring me such joy!

Coming to this simple understanding has finally released me from the "rat race" and "competition" with myself.

My Recommendations

Based on all of these experiences, ongoing education, and mentorship, I share these personal recommendations with you as you create and grow your disability-focused offering:

1. **Allow yourself grace.** Don't try to be perfect in your profession, your offering, or as a person. Identify your "weaknesses" and embrace them. This doesn't mean you don't find tools or support to help you, but don't let anything stop you from moving forward and achieving. People need you and your talents. Focus on your strengths and let them shine!

2. **Set your own metrics.** Don't let anyone define what "success" looks like for you. There isn't a magic number, location, or person that defines what your efforts are worth. Only YOU can determine why your heart beats and how effective you are with your life.

3. **Do what you love,** and it will never be "work." I can't tell you how true this is! I've completed more than 60 podcast interviews with amazing disability leaders all over the world, and this rings true for every one of them—they love what they are doing. This is the "secret sauce" you are looking for. You can help MORE people with disabilities with your specific talents, strengths, and passions!

My Wish for You

My intentions for creating this book are enormous, and I entrust my deepest wishes with you:

I hope that you find a way to support, create, and celebrate people with disabilities in every way that resonates with your soul and talents. What do I mean by this? Open your eyes and heart to the world of opportunities that continue to grow every day.

"Be the change you want to see in the world."

~ Mahatma Gandhi

This starts with seeing the needs that are already out there and finding ways that you can make an impact. It can be as simple as supporting online disability-focused fundraising efforts (via Facebook, email, Instagram, or other social media) with donations or participating in activities you enjoy, such as joining a runners' community event focused on disability awareness and support.

If you are already a part of the disability community, you may have other opportunities to be more impactful based on your strengths, experiences, and passions.

Identify your gifts and talents, and apply them. Believe in your "ripple."

My Community

Listen to my episode on the Xceptional Leaders podcast:

Why Podcasting with Mai Ling Chan

Ways to Connect with Me

Website: www.mailingchan.com

Twitter: @mailingchan

LinkedIn: @mailingchan

Facebook: @mailingchanslp

Mai Ling Chan is a speech-language pathologist, author, podcaster, business consultant, and national speaker. In addition to her position as director of growth and achievement with Cognixion, a leading AAC technology team, she also co-hosts the Xceptional Leaders Podcast *and is the CEO of* XceptionalED *and the* Xceptional Podcast Network.

From Fearful to Fearless

Advocating through Leadership, Public Speaking, and Becoming a Bestselling Author

Catherine Hughes

Photo by Jackie Carlantonio

I'm definitely my parents' daughter. Listen, I've always been a writer. I've been writing since I was in grade school, if you can believe that. I was a wee reporter for *Tiger Talk* (what, you've never heard of my elementary school newspaper?) starting in the third grade. Back in my day (heaven help me, I sound like I'm 65), I wrote for every school newspaper up through graduation, enthusiastically serving as both a reporter and as an editor. I continued with this passion through college.

At the end of my freshman year of college, I became pregnant with my one and only son, Christian, and took some time off to have him. What did I want to do when I returned to finish my associate's degree? HELLO? I wanted to return to my editor-in-chief position at the campus newspaper! I missed it terribly during my semester off.

I had no idea two decades ago that I would eventually utilize my skills as a writer, or how I would develop a passion for speaking. Building on these talents, I am currently a leader on a team supporting several states in the northeastern United States, I have published bestselling books as a coauthor and editor, and I speak to audiences from seven to 700 people.

You know that sound you hear when someone stops an old school record suddenly on the turntable? (YouTube it if you must—type in "vinyl stopping sound effect," and you're welcome.) SPEAKING?

Huh-uh! No way, no how, can't make me do it, nope, not me! *That* is how I would have reacted if you had said to me as a young single mother that I would be embracing the opportunities that I claim today in 2020. Then again, at the age of 22 (circa 2001), I had no idea that I was soon going to be drafted into an army of men and women—an army for which I was not the least bit prepared.

I became an autism warrior mother. My draft into this role was more along the lines of being taken by force, my arms dragging on the ground, scratching and clawing as I screamed, begging not to be pulled away. You see, my son did not receive his diagnosis on the autism spectrum in a typical manner—not by a long shot.

I remember exactly what I was wearing on April 19, 2001—an orange polo shirt, khaki capris, brown suede boots, and a matching brown suede button-down blazer. It was seemingly another day, another doctor's appointment. This time, it was with our endocrinologist. That day, my parents (who helped raise my son as I was a young, single mother) and I were told that Christian's tantrums as a three-year-old cherub-faced boy, his lack of language, and his peculiar behaviors couldn't just be a "boy thing." The doctor said we needed to continue to seek answers to the many questions that were surfacing.

After the appointment, my family went to get something to eat before I had to head to work. At the restaurant, we talked about scheduling follow-up appointments and other things to do, until one of Christian's outbursts drew attention.

I never made it home to call for help or make any appointments because of this phrase, "You are under arrest for terroristic threats, endangering the welfare of a minor, and simple assault on your son."

This statement was made by an officer who never read my rights. I was arrested and then jailed for four days in downtown Pittsburgh after patrons and the manager of a local restaurant watched me trying to calm my son amidst a meltdown and then remove him from the premises. They interpreted what they saw as child abuse, not once thinking "maybe this mother needs some help" or "why is this child struggling so much?"

"Child abuser." The people standing around the restaurant lobby while I was in handcuffs repeated those words in my ear, over and over again. I can still hear them if I sit silently enough.

Fast forward six weeks...

"Pervasive developmental disorder, NOS." Dr. Newman said to me.

"Wait, so . . . this is something he can grow out of, right? I can get him help? At least he's not on the spectrum. That's a relief. It's not my fault."

"Cathy . . ." he said gently. "No, this is not your fault. It's nobody's fault. But PDD-NOS . . . it is on what we call the 'spectrum.' Cathy, your son has a form of autism."

At that moment, I felt everything around me disappear, like I was sitting in an empty white room with endless walls and time and space. I felt great confusion setting in, incredible sadness for my son's future, immense anger at my pediatrician for not believing me when I asked for help as I insisted something wasn't right, and guilt for feeling a slight twinge of relief that I truly was not to blame.

"He has ... autism," I said out loud, puzzled, frightened, yet relieved all at the same time.

At the time of Christian's diagnosis, I was struggling to secure services, clear my name, and also hold down my full-time job as an assistant manager in retail so I could put food in my son's mouth and clothes on his back—not to mention budget for costs not covered by insurance for therapy-related needs and other expenses.

I didn't realize that my new role also came with SO. MANY. JOBS.

➢ Teacher
➢ Therapist
➢ Scientist
➢ Driver (to a million and ten appointments)
➢ Researcher
➢ Nutritionist
➢ Administrator
➢ Coordinator
➢ Advocate
➢ Writer
➢ Speaker

There's that damn vinyl sound again. Annoying, isn't it?

Most of those roles were tedious but came fairly easy to me, especially the writing part. I prided myself on writing powerful letters to the Independent Education Plan (IEP) team comprised of all the right lingo, providing written input for my son's applied behavior analysis treatment team complete with data and graphs, and sending tear-jerking letters with a photo of my son to legislators when we faced our first threat of losing services in Pennsylvania. I didn't travel to the state capitol with other families in 2002, not just because the travel would be difficult. I didn't think I had a loud enough voice.

Who was *I*? I was just a relatively clueless young, single mother who was winging it with this new "autism mom" gig. Is this story resonating with you? Do you feel like you don't have a strong enough voice to speak up and out? Are you not knowledgeable enough? Do you feel as if you don't have enough to offer? I felt this way too. But I was wrong. I was so very wrong.

After almost two years of procuring treatments and tools and finally reaching out for support beyond my son's therapists and teachers, I decided I wanted to give back more than what I was posting on Yahoo chat boards (2003 knew no Facebook or even MySpace, oh my!) and to fellow parents in my son's preschool placement.

"I want to give back some of what so graciously has been given to my family," is a phrase taken from my LinkedIn profile and that I have used for many biographical snapshots.

No longer wishing to return to the world of retail after a lengthy hiatus doing *ALL THE THINGS* for my son with autism, I decided to search for a position in the behavioral health field supporting families like mine that didn't require an advanced degree (as I only completed my associate's degree). I figured if I could get through someone's front door, I could develop other skills and know-how as I proved my value. I was tech-savvy, a great writer, knew the world of applied behavior analysis and other mental health services due to personal experience, and figured that was enough to find someone who would take a chance on me.

I was hired in 2003 by a growing behavioral health company in Western Pennsylvania as a parent liaison and for technical support. I managed their website content, developed a chat board, provided administrative support, and most importantly, answered the phone when families called in search of in-home services. I worked there for almost a year before I decided it was time to move on. Within a matter of weeks, I interviewed with a larger company with greater reach and a mission more aligned with what I stood for as a mother and as a "newbie advocate." I was hired as their family support coordinator within days of the interview, and soon worked my way up to director of family support services.

I worked alongside our autism team of directors and coordinators to develop resources, marketing materials, focus groups, support groups, and training courses, as well as attend conferences and workshops. I absorbed new information and also gained and homed in on skills by working closely with clinicians, administrators, and corporate leaders alike. I was like a sponge, just wanting to soak it all in! As I continued to network with other organizations and community leaders through my role, I realized I was making a name for myself. I was soon being approached to present at more support groups within the boundaries of and also outside of my position and was asked to speak in local schools, and later, I was being sought out as a presenter for workshop breakout sessions. I knew that what I was offering through my work truly strengthened my voice and raised my confidence but had no idea back then (approximately 2005) just how far I would go!

I will never forget the first time I co-presented with a colleague for our training on supporting families and siblings. I literally FELL. ON. THE. FLOOR. I didn't pass out, but I was overwhelmed with emotion because I was able to release the story inside of me for the first time in front of a room of people. I was a little shaky, sure. However, speaking for the first time made me realize: 1) this whole being in front of a crowd thing isn't so bad, and 2) I had a story to tell that impacted people who were treating families just like mine.

As I continued onward, opportunities arose such as offers to join nonprofit boards, requests to support charitable endeavors, and more. I positioned myself with like-minded people whose goals aligned with the mission of my company and my own personal philosophy. I took many chances, knowing that by continuing to learn and by continuing to speak up and out, my reach would be stronger and my voice even louder.

In 2007, I was asked to speak at a fundraising luncheon. I was nervous because it was supposed to be a large crowd—larger than I was used to with presentations to colleagues (usually 20 max) or to schools (usually groups of 50 or less). The cause was important to me, and I had many cheering me on, so I agreed. When I was called to the podium by the emcee, I felt my palms sweat and my papers shake. Once I stepped up to the podium, something came over me. I knew that my story would not only inspire people perhaps never touched by autism to join us in our efforts, but that it would spark a fire in parents and caregivers who feel like giving up.

I spoke to a room of more than 700 people that day. I received a standing ovation from a room full of people in tears, clapping and cheering loudly. That day changed my life.

In 2018, I launched my blog, *The Caffeinated Advocate* to share more of my family's journey, thoughts, and tips with a global audience. I've slowly branded myself as the mama bear on the go who always has a coffee cup in her hand and speaks her mind but often in a graceful manner. If you watch my Facebook Live broadcasts however, sometimes I'm just trying to get my viewers to crack a smile. Sometimes our lives are quite stressful, and we need a break from ASD (autism spectrum disorder) and IEP and ABCDEFG (there are seriously a lot of acronyms!). We just need to laugh!

My Gifts

In 2019, I had the opportunity to collaborate with a group of women to self-publish a collaboration of stories about our journeys through autism. Of course, I said, "yes"—actually, I dropped the phone and screamed, "YES YES YES YES, A THOUSAND TIMES YES!" I was a coauthor and also was asked to serve as the book's lead editor. After reaching bestseller status on Amazon within a matter of hours of our launch, I was hungry for more. I was living my dream! I promised my daddy, days before he passed in 2009 that I would become an author, and that I would also find a way to publish his poems. It HAPPENED!

At the time of publishing my first collaboration, I had also enrolled in two courses to further educate and empower myself. I completed Competence and Confidence—Partners in Policymaking (C2P2) with Temple University's Institute on Disabilities (Philadelphia, Pa.) and also Inspiring Lives International's six-week EmpowerU Masterclass with Dr. Shellie Hipsky. Completing both courses left me feeling more inspired and empowered than ever. I had accomplished so much for a decade-and-a half into my autism journey, but I knew I could do even more. I went on to co-author and edit two more collaborations, both of which hit best-seller prior to their launch.

I have so much in store for 2020 and beyond, and I am ecstatic. I can't wait to continue to share my message with the entire world as I move forward as a sought after author, editor, speaker, and trainer. I continue to support families, leading a team of specialists as the director of family support and community engagement at Achieving True Self, an organization serving several states in the northeast United States. I can give back to my community while also boosting my income, which supports my family. Since beginning this journey as a part-time support worker, I have *tripled* my income. I have spent the past sixteen years reaching tens of thousands of people through this calling of mine, and I am looking forward to the day that I can say I have reached millions. That day will come, mark my words.

The educational, financial, personal, and philosophical growth I've gained over the years is profound. You know what? YOU CAN DO THIS, TOO.

My Recommendations

1. **Learn all you can.** Enroll in coursework, non-credit courses, or a masterclass or find a coach. Attend workshops, conferences, and trainings. Ask questions of experts and colleagues. Follow blogs and pages that fit your niche. Maybe you will do all of the above! Align yourself with people who inspire you to cultivate your voice and your offering.

2. **Network, network, network.** See point one! It's critical to find your tribe and to connect with people—not only those who are interested in what you have to offer, but also those who can put you in front of the audience you are trying to reach.

3. **Say YES.** Now, remember—sometimes saying "yes" to too much means you are saying "no" to yourself. Don't lose yourself or sacrifice self-care in the process! My point is that you need to not fear saying "yes" to what scares you. If it scares you, I most definitely challenge you to say "yes" and not jump to "no" out of fear. Start a blog. Create a course. Speak to a large audience. Schedule a meeting with a community leader. Advocate at a rally. As Nike says, just do it!

My Wish for You

Just because you may not be the best writer, strongest speaker, or most knowledgeable advocate doesn't mean you can't learn as you go along by using the power of connection and releasing what may be some of your strongest fears. If you have the passion, you have the ability inside of you, and it is just waiting to burst.

I've overcome unbelievable obstacles and am doing my part to make this world more inclusive, more accepting, and more loving. It brings me immense joy and unbelievable satisfaction and has scaled my income to support those I love the most. It's an "exceptional" feeling.

My Community

Listen to my episode on the Xceptional Leaders podcast:

Autism Parent Takes Advocacy to the Next Level with Catherine Hughes

Ways to Connect with Me

Website:
www.thecaffeinatedadvocate.com

Facebook: @caffeinatedadvocate

Instagram: @caffeinatedadvocate

LinkedIn: @catherineahughes

Catherine Hughes is an innovative storyteller and community strategist, currently employed as the director of family support and community engagement at Achieving True Self. *Inspired by raising a son with autism, now 22 years old, she has cultivated a fascinating career spanning over 17 years, providing comprehensive support and passionate advocacy for individuals, families, and their surrounding communities. She also maintains a blog,* The Caffeinated Advocate, *and is a sought-after multiple bestselling author, editor, speaker, and trainer.*

Differently Awesome

Turning Tragedy into Purpose through Children's Disability Awareness Books

Simon Calcavecchia

I have faced many challenges in my life. One of them has been my disability. In 2002, I broke my neck playing rugby in Australia. At nineteen years old, I went from being an able-bodied person to being someone who depends on others for just about everything. However, my biggest challenge has not been my physical limitation. It has been my limited mindset.

When I first was injured, I was devastated by the amount of loss I experienced. I felt infantilized by it. Today, I need caregivers around the clock to help me with things that most people do without thinking. When I became paralyzed, all of my dreams vanished. I had to start my life over. My identity as a person was changed forever.

To begin my new life with quadriplegia, I had to accept the things I could not change. Acceptance was the key to finding passion in my life and discovering that I had a greater purpose.

After coming home from the hospital, I decided that the best thing I could do with my life was return to school. In 2009, I graduated from The Evergreen State College (Olympia, Wash.) with a bachelor of arts degree. Unfortunately, following my graduation, I had a hard time finding a job. It was really depressing. It didn't help that I lacked confidence due to my physical limitations and didn't have enough experience to truly believe in myself. I decided to change that and started volunteering with kids.

In 2010, I began volunteering in elementary schools and at the Children's Museum in Olympia. When I volunteered with children, I knew I was making a difference, not just in their lives but in mine, too. Volunteering filled my life in all kinds of ways. Most importantly, it gave me the confidence to believe in myself. That alone catalyzed my creative drive. Ultimately, it led me to my career as a children's book author and motivational speaker.

In 2016, after seven years of volunteering with kids, I embarked on a journey that was as transformative for my life as the day I became paralyzed. It all happened after I met my good friend, Arturo Alvarez. We met in Olympia during an art project for the Procession of the Species. The event celebrates the largest annual Earth Day in the Pacific Northwest. The celebration includes the Luminary Light Festival, costumes, and giant floats. When I heard about the event, I knew I had to test out my confidence by creating a team of supporters who would help me build a float for the Procession. After five weeks, I went from having zero knowledge of how to build a float to building one of the biggest floats in the parade. Our team of 50 people created a Komodo dragon the size of a bus, which we mounted on my wheelchair. The incredible experience of driving the float through the streets of downtown Olympia taught me how to become a leader. It also gave me the confidence I needed to manifest an even bigger dream.

For many years, I dreamt of making my own children's book series. I loved the idea of writing stories for children. It is a craft so close to my heart. However, it was still a distant reality. I had no idea where to begin. That's when Arturo came into the picture. Two years into our friendship, I discovered that he had a hidden talent for illustration. I will never forget the time when we were sitting at my dining room table and he randomly showed me a doodle of a funny cartoon character. When I saw it, I knew instantly that he was the right person to help me turn my dream into reality. It was something that just felt right. It also inspired both of us to create something that had the power to make a positive difference in the world. During the first year, we met two or three times a week to create our first published children's book. By the end of that year, we had made something special.

Publishing our first book was a fun challenge, but the hardest part was yet to come. We had to find a way to get them into the hands of our readers. After the first book was released, I had to turn the book into a successful business. As the author, success mostly depended on me. That meant that I had to become an entrepreneur, a salesman, a marketer, and a social media expert. How could I possibly do all that with zero experience as well as having quadriplegia? It was a tough question to answer. In my reality, I depend on others for my independence from getting up in the morning to having someone drive me where I want to go, I need a lot of help in my life. However, I did have one thing going for me. I believed in myself!

To be successful, I had to figure out a way to reach my audience. I wanted to share my message of inclusion, positive mindset, and disability awareness with as many children as possible. I decided to become an assembly speaker and visit schools. That way I could share my story with five hundred kids at a time. To do that, I knew finding a mentor would be vital. As I developed my ideas, I reached out to a principal at an elementary school where I used to volunteer. He was very supportive. We started talking about my presentation and how to engage the kids with different mediums. I made videos about my life at home with quadriplegia. I taught kids about rugby. I made a highlight reel of some of my YouTube adventures to show kids what it means to live life with a positive mindset. Before I knew it, I had created a presentation that was ready for my first school visit.

In 2016, I visited my first school, Hansen Elementary in Olympia. It was an unforgettable experience. I could see the impact I was making, and my dream had turned into something much greater than my own personal goals of success. The obstacles that I faced were no longer as important as the impact that I could make. That was the moment when I realized I was meant to change the world.

In all of the years I volunteered with kids, I didn't find one book in the classroom that had a character using a wheelchair. With that realization, I had found my purpose, and it became my responsibility to change that.

Representation matters! Now I go into school after school asking the librarians about stories that have characters with disabilities. Most of them have very few, if any. If you didn't know, there are 50 million people in the United States that live with a disability. Most of them do not see themselves in movies, books, or stories about being superheroes. We need to create more representation to teach kids messages of inclusion, acceptance, and inspiration.

I will never forget the day that a young boy came up to me after I gave an assembly presentation at an elementary school. He was beaming with excitement. I asked him what he thought of the assembly. He replied by saying, "I thought that the assembly was awesome. I have autism, and it finally feels like I have someone on my side." When I heard that, it broke my heart. However, it is the fuel that drives me to make a difference. I want everyone to feel like they have someone on their side.

I personally know what it feels like to be treated differently. Some people have yelled out of their car windows at me, they have murmured unkind words under their breath as they pass me in the streets, and at times, I have been treated as an inferior person just because I have a disability. That is why I am driven to be successful.

My Gifts

The most important thing that I have gained from my personal experience with quadriplegia has been to believe in myself. Before I became an author, I didn't know what I was capable of. Now, I know that I can turn my dreams into reality.

Becoming a motivational speaker was one of the best things to ever happen to me. Not only has it provided me with a career, but it has also given me a purpose. It has helped me make a positive difference in this world by sharing my story.

Due to my financial success as an author and a speaker, I have been approved by the Department of Vocational Rehabilitation for my first vehicle. I will finally be able to drive myself in 2020. I haven't done that in eighteen years.

My Recommendations

In the 18 years that I have lived my life with paralysis, I have been able to grow into the person I have always wanted to be. I have done that by living my life with a positive mindset by focusing on the "can" and not the "cannot." My recommendations are meant to inspire you to find your own path to making a positive difference.

1. **Say "yes" to new opportunities.**

2. **Try anything that has the potential to bring passion into your life.** You never know how it will be useful down the road.

3. **Take action!** Action is the most important thing you can do.

4. **Collaborate.** Teamwork leads to dream work.

5. **Learn from others.** When you find a passion, find a mentor.

My Wish for You

If I could teach you anything, then it would be to believe in yourself. To discover your passions and let them lead you to your purpose. Anything is possible when you believe in yourself.

Regardless of whether you are living with a disability, it is important to recognize when we make excuses in our lives. For many years, I made the excuse that I wasn't capable because of my disability. It took a lot of experimenting with new things to discover that I am more capable than I ever imagined. Don't ever let your excuses stop you from living your dreams.

My Community

Listen to my episode on the Xceptional Leaders podcast:

Inspiring and Encouraging Through Children's Books with Simon Calcavecchia

Ways to Connect with Me

Website:
www.frankandmustard.com

Twitter: @FrankandMustard

Facebook: @FrankandMustard

LinkedIn: @SimonCalcavecchia

Instagram: @Frank and Mustard

Amazon: *The Adventures of Frank and Mustard*

YouTube: The Adventures of Frank and Mustard

In 2002, Simon Calcavecchia moved to Australia to follow his dream of playing rugby. After his third game of the season, he was injured in a scrum leaving him with c5/6 quadriplegia. Now, Simon has become a children's book author and a motivational speaker. He visits schools to teach a story of perseverance, growth mindset, and acceptance of others.

Spark On!

Finding your Spark and the Spark in Others on the Path to Successful Employment

Angela Mahoney

M Ed

It was 2006. I was 26 years young, married to my soulmate, and seven months pregnant with our first son. I was so tired. In addition to preparing for motherhood, I was also working full-time as a special educator in a private setting, teaching middle and high school students with a range of physical and educational needs. My passions were teaching, my classroom, and my students. I also worked social, weekend overnight, and school-based sporting events with my students because *they filled my soul.* Additionally, I was on my way to becoming a published author. I was living the life I dreamed of having, paired, ironically, with a sense that it was all going by a bit too quickly, and that I may be perpetually tired for the next 20 years.

Flashback to three years before, to 2003, when I was in my third year of teaching—I was highly aware of the uniquely rare school I was blessed to be a part of. It was the kind of learning environment every child deserves. Even the educators were afforded opportunities to learn, grow, and succeed. When obstacles arose, a team of "helpers" problem-solved together. They had a true hands-on approach to student growth and development. Because of this environment, I had grown as an educator and, quite honestly, as a human too, in just the short time I had experienced teaching in the classroom.

During this time I worked alongside a range of remarkable team members with various skills and specialties. One colleague in particular, Lynn Stoller, was an occupational therapist who saw value in the work I created for the students I taught daily. She saw the real-life application, as well as long-term benefits of the established, system-focused curriculum I had created in my classroom. One day, after a group session together, Lynn pulled me aside, and we talked for a few minutes.

"Angie, this work you are doing is really unique!" Lynn said.

"Oh stop, Lynn, you know it's how teachers roll," I replied, shying away from the attention. "I appreciate you seeing my focus."

"No, really, have you thought about publishing this? There is such a need for this focus and these skills" she added.

"Publish? Wow, that thought seriously never crossed my mind!" I began feeling excited, and then uncertain, and then excited again. "Do you really think this is worthy?"

I remember this moment vividly as something was unexpectedly sparked in me, something I never thought possible of myself or even considered. Until this moment.

This was my first of many sparks!

After my initial reaction, suddenly, my thinking shifted. I *knew* this was worthy work designed to help others beyond my small classroom in Massachusetts. My mental wheels turned as my colleague suggested a publisher she had worked with. She shared their contact information, and immediately, I reached out, eager to connect, not knowing one smidge about publishing or being an author. I had done so much work already with the curriculum in my classroom. How hard could it be? I soon would find out.

Now, let's flash forward and return to the image of a tired 26-year-old, third-trimester pregnant, full-time teaching woman who is coming quickly to her deadline for her first publication to be complete. This deadline includes front-to-back, edit-to-edit, visual-to-visual completion. I am in full panic mode. I am ready to quit. To let go of the daily dreams and visions I had of the work I created to help so many. I knew it was crunch time. I tried to cope, but, admittedly, I was in over my head in uncharted seas.

I had spent the last few months collaborating with the publishing team, and the curriculum was really coming together. I wanted to give so much energy to the project, but I was struggling to find the time. I knew if I hit the "pause" button on the project to adjust to my new mommy world, I would be in dangerous territory, possibly never returning to the dream of being an author.

This felt like a crossroads in my life. My challenge was creating the balance I struggled to strike between focusing on my career and focusing on motherhood. I had come to this point as the reality of time and energy, or lack thereof, were weighing on me daily. When I began to feel unwell in the eighth month of my pregnancy, I was placed on bed rest. I realized then it was time to slow down. I was forced to listen to my mind and body (not always a strength of mine). It was not my time to powerhouse through all of my dreams the quick way. I needed to hit "pause" on the publishing project with a passionate persistence to return to this dream in my lifetime, a promise I needed to keep to myself.

As expected, this "pause" was needed and necessary. I am glad I listened to my inner voice at that time, as challenging and scary as it felt. I am now a happily married 40-year-old mom of two boys, still tired (but sleeping more each day), maintaining a full-time role in the classroom. It took seven years (yes 7!) of deliberate focus and growth as a mother and a teacher to get back to the publishing project. And, although my timeline with the publishers shifted, my five-module work skills curriculum was published in 2013! My work was finally out in the world, and I knew this was just the beginning of helping so many find their spark!

My Inspiration

I knew at a young age I wanted to be a teacher. When I was a little girl, I set up a classroom in my bedroom with all of my stuffed animals as students. I loved to be a leader and enjoyed being at the front of the room demanding quiet (I have lovely video as proof). Yes, feisty 6-year-old me.

Fortunately for me, my remarkable mother, a special education teacher, embraced this passion I had for education. She took me to her classroom as often as she could, and introduced me to her unique students, highlighting their greatest attributes. In the classroom, my mom lit up, and in my early elementary years, I knew I wanted to light up, too. *I wanted that spark.*

By middle school, my family settled into a new home in a cute country town in Connecticut. Like most middle-schoolers, I was still awkwardly uncomfortable in my own skin and really disliked my curly hair—the usual 13-year-old challenges. I began to find that schoolwork and lessons moved too quickly for me, and I was not able to keep up. Daily (and into the night), my patient mom would help me with my homework, giving me study tips and encouraging me to stay focused. We continued to work together for my schooling success, and I thankfully survived the middle school years with very little damage.

High school brought new challenges. Although I had wonderful friendships with classmates and teammates, I experienced many learning ups and downs, and, during these years, I was diagnosed with ADHD. Instead of feeling unhappy about that news, I felt relieved—at least now I had an answer to why I felt so frustrated with my learning abilities. Once I was placed in the correct classes and received the right support, I began to flourish. I experienced first-hand how a teacher can guide your education and again *felt a spark* that education was my calling.

Planning to attend college with the intention of becoming a special educator filled me with a greater sense of purpose. I soaked up my college years in Cambridge, Mass., and benefited from the small, all-women setting. I found myself immersed in conversations that brought my level of thinking and understanding to a whole new level. When I graduated in 2003 with my master's, I was ready to jump into the real world. I accepted a teaching position as a work-skills instructor in a small private school. I could not wait to have my own classroom and to be in service to what I truly believed was my calling to work in the area of special education.

In my first few years as a teacher, I began to evaluate what curriculum and lessons were in place, as well as what was needed to help my students grow in my focus area of work readiness skills. I quickly realized that programs to support employment for various learners with unique needs were lacking. I started creating lessons and visual materials to help my students prepare for vocational opportunities in the community. Almost immediately, I saw the benefits these pre-workplace lessons and activities were having on my students: less anxiety, greater confidence, and openness to try new things. I could see the spark lighting up m*y students*, and I was creating opportunities for those sparks.

Helping ALL individuals feel a sense of purpose and worth is what drove me as an educator then and continues to do so for me today as I help many individuals worldwide create and implement systems to prepare for successful employment futures.

My Gifts

Years ago, I ran into a former student when I was shopping at a local grocery store. I couldn't believe that this young man I taught in middle school who like many of my students, faced a unique set of learning challenges—was now a high school graduate with a job.

As soon as we began talking, I could see his pride and confidence shining through as he bagged my groceries. As I turned to leave, he shared that he remembered learning how to bag groceries in my class. I couldn't believe it. That moment, *that spark,* solidified my purpose for educating professionals and parents about pre-vocational training and underscored my passion for helping all individuals find their spark. That's my gift.

As an educator, I have the beautiful opportunity to see so many successes daily, some small and others big, but each bringing joy. I relish seeing my students grow into confident, prepared young adults, eager to continue to discover their new-found purpose. These moments are reminders of how my gift has helped others. My gift is seeing uniqueness in so many, uncovering an alternative way to approach or access a situation, and creating a way to give all a voice on their vocational journey to the workforce.

Since publishing the modules of pre-vocational lessons and hands-on activities in 2013, I have been fortunate to connect with individuals daily and continue to share the many ways vocational foundations can be established and encouraged in a variety of settings. I am amazed by the many shapes the curriculum has taken on, as well as the range of ways it is helping so many diverse users. Educators, therapists, and parents on a mission are truly game-changers and use their drive to change societal norms, as well as expectations. It is truly uplifting to work with so many of these individuals as we all continue to focus on making the world a better place.

My Recommendations

Based on all of these experiences, ongoing education, and mentorship, I share these personal recommendations with you as you create and grow your disability-focused offering:

1. **Listen to your inner voice.** If something feels rushed or off, honor that it might be. If the timing seems tricky, pause to see why, and ask what changes can be made. If a request or a project is too large, break it down into smaller, digestible bites. Do not be afraid to hit the "pause" button at any time in your life. The crossroads

will come and go, and the path you choose will matter, so take the time to listen.

2. **Embrace your gifts.** Shout them loudly off rooftops and out of car windows. Wear your strengths like a golden, diamond-encrusted crown. Often, reflecting and proudly stating our gifts is not a natural thing but, gosh darn it, it should be! What you bring to any table is rare, and the world needs your uniqueness, your take on any situation, your approach to any challenge, and your lenses on a range of topics. With you being your best self, you ultimately help others be their best, sparkling selves, too.

3. **Journal, journal, journal.** Have a notebook handy on this journey. Take time daily to focus on your strengths, your goals, the steps you need to take and/or are taking toward them, recent connections and networking opportunities, as well as ideas that have come to mind, yes at 2 a.m.! Create a vision board, and go BIG! Create a visual way to see your idea, product, or dream come to life! By writing and visually laying it out, you will believe it can really happen (because it really can, friend!).

4. **Acknowledge things, people, and situations that ignite your spark.** Recognize moments that resonate with you, people who encourage you to take a look at the work you are doing, and ideas that continue to come to you, especially in the middle of the night. These are small sparks that can lead to big, successful fires. You have the potential, the worth, and the drive. Just be sure to stay open to the flow of these concepts

to allow for continued growth and development in all areas you tackle in your future.

5. **Share your story with the world.** Networking and social media are your friends! Put yourself and your work out there. Create a page where others can follow you. Write blogs and articles to share on social media. Join podcasts to broaden your audience. Develop webinars to help your idea reach people around the world. You have access to the world at your fingertips! If these are areas you are unsure of, challenge yourself to learn more and try one small, but consistent, step. As you see the interest grow, take the next step.

My Wish for You

"It's very hard to have ideas. It's very hard to put yourself out there, it's very hard to be vulnerable, but those people who do that are the dreamers, the thinkers, and creators. They are the magic people of the world."

~ Amy Poehler

In these fast-paced times, it can be challenging to feel authentic, influential, and magical. Feeling as though the work you do makes a difference, is seen, is recognized can be tough. Many times we go through the day-to-day motions and settle for ease over challenge and a smidge of discomfort. My wish for you is to understand that *you are what the world needs*. Recognize the times you are sparked to do something more, something bigger, and the times you are called to help others see their spark!

My Community

Listen to my episode on the Xceptional Leaders podcast:

Building Strong Foundation Employment Skills with Angela Mahoney

Ways to Connect with Me

Facebook: Spark On Spark Others

Website: http://icanwork.therapro.com/

LinkedIn: www.linkedin.com/in/icanwork

Email: angelamahoneymed@gmail.com

Angela Mahoney, M.Ed., is an educator, vocational planning consultant, and internationally known author whose career has focused on helping diverse individuals find their spark on the path to successful employment. She serves as a teacher, advisor, curriculum developer, and trainer, where she is the founding expert on building an individually focused work-readiness foundation for all.

Mahoney holds a B.S. in special education and human development studies as well as a master's degree in intensive special needs from Lesley University (Cambridge, Mass.).

Part II: Stronger Together

New Housing and Community Models for Autism

A Parent's Journey Toward a More Promising Future

Denise D. Resnik

Photo by Sydnee Schwartz

I worried about the health of my children long before college, marriage, and pregnancy. It dated back to my early days as a ventriloquist, entertaining kids with physical and developmental disabilities. Their parents struggled with what to do, where to go—and so many whys. I was barely ten years old at the time, leaving those group homes, centers, and hospitals struggling with my own doubts about whether I could be a good mother to a child with so many challenges.

When Matt was born in 1991, I promptly counted his ten fingers and toes and then sighed with great relief at his 9.6 Apgar score. Daughter Ally, born just 17 months earlier, was thriving. Our prayers had been answered!

But something changed after Matt's first birthday. He stopped looking at us and responding to his name. The pediatrician said not to worry. The audiologist reported perfect hearing. Before I saw more specialists, my mother gave me a book titled, Let Me Hear Your Voice. I only had to read the first few chapters to know what I so wanted to deny: Our son has autism.

What I experienced next was the kind of pain for which there is no relief. The kind that sent me into the forest of Northern Arizona on the first of many long runs, wailing like an animal that had lost her cub.

After Matt's official diagnosis in 1993, our dreams for him and our family vanished. We were told institutionalization would be best. Such was the prevailing counsel for this confounding disorder impacting one in 2,500 U.S. children at the time.

Following the creation of our home-based, intensive one-on-one therapy program, my husband and I wrestled with Matt's future and the possibilities of supporting him at home for as long as possible. We also explored our options. I'll never forget what I saw, smelled, and felt in those places— and all the memories it uncovered from my childhood. I also pledged to find a better place where Matt could live his adult life and we, as his parents, could find peace of mind.

Thankfully, much has changed since Matt's autism diagnosis. Back then, we didn't know where to go or what to do. We barely knew what autism was. The landscape was barren and the internet just emerging. I connected with a small support group of mothers who met at a coffee shop near the local mall. We were all focused on the pressing questions of the day. One table of moms became two, then four—until we filled an entire restaurant with moms *and* dads.

We pursued answers and remedies everywhere. Intensive early intervention and applied behavioral analysis therapy. Vitamins. Pork hormones. Some therapies were supported by data—others not—including those that gave us hope to help our children sleep, eat, or stop chewing the leather on our living room couches.

The really big questions always loomed: *How did this happen? Will he recover? Am I to blame? How can I be the mom he needs and deserves when there's so much I don't know and so much I fear?*

We started to find answers in our Phoenix community of friends, families, physicians, and professionals. With their help, and quite humbly, the Southwest Autism Research & Resource Center (SARRC) was founded in 1997. Without money, staff, or dedicated office space, we still had big dreams and a bold vision: to advance discoveries and support individuals impacted by autism and their families throughout their lifetimes.

We believed that if SARRC focused on what was right for our families and the community at large, we could create a model for communities everywhere. Today, SARRC is 200 employees strong with a $16 million annual operating budget, serves as an international model, and represents one of the most robust sites in North America for the recruitment and enrollment of subjects in pharmaceutical trials. Together, we have built a city that offers early identification, intervention, and education; lifelong learning; training and employment; a responsive, supportive community; and now more home options—all reasons why *PBS NewsHour* dubbed Phoenix "the most autism-friendly city in the world."[3]

Thanks to SARRC and our supportive community, the stage was set in 2012 for the founding of First Place AZ, SARRC's sister nonprofit and a residential and community developer responding to that looming question: Who will care for my child when I'm no longer able?

While my knees now preclude those long runs in the forest, I've been on a marathon of sorts in search of answers for more than two decades. Autism is currently diagnosed in one in 54 children in the United States. Approximately 60,000

---

[3] "First Place Phoenix news page." Shared from PBS NewsHour. https://www.firstplaceaz.org/about/news/

of them are also transitioning to adulthood annually, faced with a bleak landscape of confusing, fragmented, or nonexistent services where unemployment or underemployment hovers at around 86 percent.

Backed by 20-plus years of research, more than 100 collaborators, and support from the Urban Land Institute, First Place AZ is positioned for transformational impact on how society approaches housing and community development for individuals with autism and other neurodiversities.

We're realizing this vision through our first major project, First Place–Phoenix, a $15.4 million, 81,000-square-foot property set in the heart of the urban area and designed for 79 people as a place for living and learning through its three primary components: 1) First Place Apartments, where residents enjoy a suite of supports, property amenities, and a robust community life with all the benefits of connected, urban living: transportation, healthcare, employment, continuing education, and recreation; 2) First Place Transition Academy, where students learn independent living skills through a residential program of 32 semester-length courses taught at a local community college—then practice daily what they learn in the supportive "community classroom" that is Metro Phoenix; and 3) First Place Global Leadership Institute, which serves as the catalyst for advancing replicable options and where families, people with diverse abilities, professionals, and thought leaders collaborate on housing and community solutions through training, education, research, and public policy.

Consider that we are today with options for special populations where senior housing was more than 50 years ago. We have a burgeoning market in need of homes and services that must transcend outdated and limited models. We are focused on matching the interests and needs of members of these populations with the right property location, design, and amenities—rooted in communities everywhere. A new generation of dynamic housing models is possible only by collectively tapping private, public, philanthropic, and nonprofit interests.

Together, we are advancing a bold vision by building a new marketplace that ensures housing and community options for people with autism and other neurodiversities are as bountiful as they are for everyone else. Now, when an individual or family receives that daunting diagnosis, we not only want them to access promising intervention therapies, we want them to experience places where people are thriving— with friends, jobs, healthcare, a supportive community, and opportunities to learn at any age. We want them to have hope!

My Inspiration

While Matt, now 29, is our North Star, Ally, now 30 and a wonderful mother herself, also shines brightly. We never wanted Ally to have the responsibility of replacing us as Matt's parents. I also knew we couldn't build our definition of community just for him—that we needed a wider, more inclusive lens:

Community is not just a geographic location but an emotional connection, too. It's defined by those you care about and trust to care about you. It's where you can be yourself and experience life, knowing there are always people in your corner.

Community building is a process. It requires vision, passion, grit, resilience, and an ability to connect dots—lots of them. It also requires sound strategies, which we've been developing with families across the country in ever-increasing numbers through the First Place Global Leadership Institute (https://www.firstplaceaz.org/leadership-institute/overview/).
An exciting Leadership Institute initiative now underway is *A Place in the World*—sister study to 2009's groundbreaking *Opening Doors report*—to create the foundational nomenclature for housing and service delivery models with the goal of further defining market segments, establishing best practices and guiding principles, and driving crucial collaborations that address pressing needs brought about by the housing crisis.

Although Matt is an adult, that doesn't change our incessant worrying or ongoing diligence in helping him learn and grow. He works at his own business, SMILE Biscotti (https://www.smilebiscotti.com/), volunteers for causes we all support, participates in community life as a resident of First Place, and hosts dinners for his neighbors several times a week. Yet, we still work hard to help him remember to untie his shoes before slipping them on, adjust the water temperature in the shower, take off his sweatshirt in the heat of the day, expand his limited selection of food, and tell us how he's feeling or where it hurts.

I know kids and adults with autism continue to learn at every age—and so do we as parents. Sure, there are times I think we could just sequester this sweet, innocent young man who has never done a mean thing to anyone in his entire life in our home and protect him from the outside world. We could continue enjoying his playful spirit, his singing lines from "Zipa-Dee-Doo-Dah" first thing in the morning and his cold feet in the middle of the night when he occasionally slips into our bed to snuggle. But we know that's not what's best for Matt's continued development and personal growth. During our lifetimes, we want to ensure that Matt's life beyond the family home is the very best it can be.

My Gifts

I'm an entrepreneur and a dreamer. While those are valued gifts, my most cherished are good health, my "keeper" husband Rob of 36 years, supportive family members and friends, super-smart and talented colleagues, generous donors—and a big vision to keep me going. Together, we've gotten through some very long days, even longer nights and— the longest of all—that list of "Nos." No, not a good idea. No, not now. No, not something we could support. But with each disappointing "no," we continue to embrace that big vision that picks us up, dusts us off and channels our energies in more positive directions.

I'm also a fixer. The past decade gave rise to more kids with autism than ever transitioning to adulthood. And because of the National Autism Indicators Reports (https://drexel.edu/autismoutcomes/publications-and-reports/nat-autism-indicators-report/), we have solid data indicating that the majority slide backward at a far greater rate after high school than any other disability group. We cannot allow this trend to continue in light of all the progress we've made through ever-earlier diagnosis/intervention and education. And we cannot expect disappointing, subpar results to change unless we change our approaches, practices, and communities. That's why I doubled down and dedicated my time and energy, as well as substantial resources from my marketing firm, to the creation of SARRC and First Place. I'm fortunate to have the support of extraordinary family members, friends, and colleagues, and I'm comfortable playing various roles—whether front and center, by someone's side, or behind the scenes.

My Wish for You

Find your own North Star to guide you. So many things are possible when we begin our story with a vision bigger than ourselves and keep going courageously and collectively, creating new hopes and dreams for the underserved, underrepresented, and underestimated.

Continue looking up and out for answers and direction as you ponder this compelling statement attributed to Michelangelo: "The greatest danger for most of us is not that our aim is too high and we miss it, but that it is too low and we reach it."

Learn valuable lessons, recognize who's in your corner—or on your block—and do what's attainable *now* as you plan for what's next. And remember that sometimes "No, not a good idea, not now, not something we could support" is just the start of the conversation!

My Recommendations

1. **Build your team and know who's in your corner.** Over time, expand that corner, host gatherings of those who care as much as you do, and give more people more reasons to collaborate and celebrate.

2. **Consider the "shiny object" approach.** In the same way that we would send Matt to school with a cool, new toy to encourage the other kids to notice him and play with him during recess, consider what will attract others to your vision and mission. What can you do together that you cannot do on your own that will attract and engage stellar leaders and doers?

3. **Other important lessons** we've learned along the way are shared in a series of blogs on the First Place AZ website (https://www.firstplaceaz.org/):

   - Build a trusted team that can agree—and agree to disagree
     (https://www.firstplaceaz.org/blog/2018/08/)
   - Invest early in research and discovery to inform your vision (https://www.firstplaceaz.org/blog/2018/08/)
   - No one-size-fits-all approach
     (https://www.firstplaceaz.org/blog/2018/09/)
   - Don't fall in love with or marry your plan too soon
     (https://www.firstplaceaz.org/blog/2018/10/)
   - Timeouts aren't just for kids
     (https://www.firstplaceaz.org/blog/2018/10/)

These recommendations may also be helpful:

1. **Connect.** Get out of the "silo mentality"—a barrier-building reluctance to share information—and organize by needs, interests, and complementary strengths, not solely by diagnosis. Where possible, focus on integrated, multi-level, multi-agency, and multi-generational diversity that produces richer experiences

for everyone and supports a life trajectory versus a specific destination. This kind of connection encourages change and growth.

2. **Reach out.** Involve the broader community—not just the special needs community—in addressing pressing issues. Building community support is essential for continuity of care and important life transitions.

3. **Scaffold.** Identify and evaluate what's already working in your community. Build and expand on your community's assets. Collaboration, models, and replication are all needed to create greater long-term equity, impact, and sustainability.

4. **Innovate.** Engage public, private, and charitable interests to learn what's working and what's not. Consider how to work together to avoid perpetuating old models with less-than-desirable outcomes.

5. **Measure.** Support the creation of new metrics to track value and quality of life outcomes. Only through joint efforts, data collection, and the collaboration of trusted champions can public policy advances be made.

6. **Lead by example.** The best way to change adverse statistics for adults with autism and other neurodiversities is to work together, innovate, demonstrate success, and open more doors for people looking for jobs, homes, social networks, and supportive communities.

My Community

Listen to my episode on the Xceptional Leaders podcast:

Life Awaits for Adults with Autism with Denise Resnik

Ways to Connect with Me

Website: www.firstplaceaz.org and www.autismcenter.org (SARRC)

Facebook: @FirstPlaceAZ

Twitter: @FirstPlaceAZ

LinkedIn: @FirstPlaceAZ

Instagram: @FirstPlaceAZ

An international leader in autism and native Phoenician, Denise D. Resnik is the founder and president/CEO of First Place® AZ (established in 2012), co-founder of the Southwest Autism Research & Resource Center (SARRC, established in 1997), and founder and CEO of DRA Collective (http://www.dracollective.com/), a marketing/communications firm (established in 1986) that serves clients in a variety of fields, including real estate, economic development, healthcare, education, and hospitality.

Computing the Future

A Mom Presumes Competence and Creates Limitless Opportunities

Yudi Bennett

Photo by Benjamin Schneider

If I have one main strength, it is perseverance. I don't give up. I've been thrown from a horse at least three times—even broke a wrist once—but every time I get back on. Call me crazy but I always hang on till the job is done.

In September 2011, a group of parents and professionals (including me) opened a school called Exceptional Minds in Sherman Oaks, Calif. We had nine students, four part-time instructors, ten computers, and very little money. Our goal was to train young adults to work in visual effects in the movie industry. They would need to learn the complex software used in rotoscoping, a technique for tracing movie images frame by frame to then alter or composite them. This is a tough skill for anyone to master, but here's the catch . . . our students all had autism. They had communication difficulties, sensory issues, and limited social skills. NO ONE had ever done anything like this. Most adults with autism work in menial jobs or not at all. We had no model to follow; we were "inventing the wheel."

Opening the school was premature and a half-baked idea, but we could not wait. We were desperate parents, and our teenage kids were growing up fast. Their future was a bleak one of unemployment and poverty.

Everything went fairly smoothly the first week. We had classes daily from 10 a.m. to 4 p.m. and dealt with the occasional student meltdown. I was a volunteer at the time, serving as administrator, operations manager, and jack-of-all-trades. I organized the program, dealt with vendors and families, and made sure the staff got paid. I would later take a staff position, and then join the board of directors. Our students were excited to have a place to go each morning and to develop essential technical skills. The teaching staff was hard at work creating curriculum and lesson plans, as well as delivering hands-on instruction. The parents were thrilled. For many of them, it was the first time they had hope for the future. Inside our tiny one-room school, the atmosphere was charged with positive energy.

Then the bomb fell. Our landlord—who was donating the studio space—told us he needed his storefront back, and we had to vacate. Worse yet, he gave us two weeks to move. We had to somehow rent a new space, furnish it, get it outfitted with internet access and computers, and move our students—all in two weeks and without disrupting classes! I had a moment of total panic and despair. We were at the beginning of the school year. Should I just refund each family's tuition and close shop? We were so close to helping these young adults realize their dreams. Was this to be the end?

I reminded myself that prior to this endeavor, I spent 25 years in the movie industry as an assistant director. I traveled all over the world, filming in snow, rain, and intense cold and heat. In one movie, a mansion we were about to film burned to the ground the day before we got there. I survived hurricanes and blizzards and was once trapped by a flash flood. I even survived a few actors who refused to come out of their motorhomes. But, as they say, the show must go on. In every case, creative problem-solving saved the day. Stay calm, I told myself, and look for a viable solution.

Low and behold, the solution came in the form of my lifelong friend, Susie Zwerman. Susie had been a top location scout for 20 years in the movie industry. A call to her produced several properties to check out. We quickly chose the best one, negotiated a lease, hit the second-hand stores for affordable furnishings, and got our amazing board of directors to load up their cars and move our computers while the teachers took the students on a field trip! We did not lose even one day of classes and made the move within the allotted two weeks. With that inauspicious beginning, we developed a ground-breaking vocational program in animation and visual effects for adults with autism.

My Inspiration

The movie business is all-consuming. Long hours, travel to distant locations, and constant stress all take their toll. For me, it meant delaying having a family. By the time I found the world's best husband, I had trouble getting pregnant. Finally, after five years, my son Noah was born in 1997. Everything checked out—ten fingers, ten toes, sweet smile. We were sent home with a wonderful, healthy boy.

One of my favorite Yiddish sayings is "Man plans, and God laughs." When Noah was approaching three years old, we started to look at preschools. Suddenly, he stopped talking. One day he was saying "mom" and "dad"; the next day it was "mmmm" and "dddd." We were frantic. What was wrong with our darling boy? Two months and about a dozen visits with various doctors—neurologists, psychiatrists, psychologists, developmental pediatricians—Noah was diagnosed with autism. I sat down and cried for several weeks. My husband, Bob, ever the clear-headed thinker, started researching anything he could find about autism.

The internet was in its infancy, about four books had been published on autism, and the current autism "epidemic" was just beginning. Families receiving the autism diagnosis were panicking. No one seemed to know how to help these children, and medical intervention was experimental and expensive. My husband and I got together with a few families and founded the Foothill Autism Alliance (FAA), a nonprofit organization dedicated to educating parents and helping them find resources. Each month, we brought in speakers who were experts in autism and/or related fields. These family resource meetings were open to the public and free of charge.

Even as we were busy helping other families, Bob and I started wondering what Noah's future would look like. Would he go to college, make friends, have a career, get married? We couldn't find any answers. At times, I worried that he would not survive elementary school. We were battling the local school district to get basic services for Noah such as intense speech and behavioral therapy. It broke my heart to see how isolated Noah was and how much he struggled.

Then, suddenly, Bob was diagnosed with lymphoma. Our already fragile world was shattered. He endured endless rounds of chemo, a stem cell transplant, and every other treatment that promised even a single ray of hope. I kept working in the film industry to keep us afloat, and Bob took care of Noah in addition to fighting this horrific disease. Nothing seemed to help. In 2003, Bob lost his battle with cancer, and I became an unwitting single mom.

As Noah grew older, the questions about his future became more basic. He struggled academically, especially in math. Would he finish high school? Get a job? Live independently? I stopped working to help him full-time. Thanks to some dedicated teachers and talented therapists, Noah received his high school diploma in 2014. We were ecstatic!

Throughout this time, I kept looking for vocational programs but found almost none. Even the kids who managed to graduate college seemed to be unemployed and struggling. Today we know that 80% of adults with autism never move out of their parents' homes. We also know that 80–90% of adults with autism are unemployed or under-employed. We created Exceptional Minds to change this paradigm, to help adults with autism have meaningful careers and lead productive lives. Noah was, is, and will always be my inspiration!

My Gifts

I grew up in a Jewish household that fostered a strong sense of *tikkun olam*. Literally, this means "repair the world." I believe that we each have a responsibility to help make our world a better place. I was fortunate to spend my early years in the film industry honing my leadership and managerial skills. As an assistant director, I handled all the scheduling and logistics and ran the set on major studio films. I was responsible for keeping projects on schedule and on budget. As one of the first women to make a living in this capacity, I became a role model and mentored many young women who were trying to get into this field. It was my way of giving back.

Working in the nonprofit arena has also given me an opportunity to give back. Creating Foothill Autism Alliance and then Exceptional Minds has allowed me to help dozens of families and individuals by providing education, resources, and skills. It has been a life-enriching journey. I have witnessed families making incredible sacrifices for their children. I have seen volunteers donate countless hours to help out. And I have been fortunate to receive funding for these projects from incredibly generous individuals.

Foothill Autism Alliance recently celebrated its 20th anniversary. Many of the original families are still with us, part of a close-knit community. I've heard parents say that they were "drowning, and FAA saved our lives." Hearing this gives me the inspiration to continue.

At Exceptional Minds, I have seen our graduates get full-time employment, move out of their parents' homes and into their own apartments, and start living independent lives. We have partnered with industry giants such as Marvel Studios, Nickelodeon, and Cartoon Network. Our artists now see their names on the big screen, on films such as *Avengers: End Game*, *Black Panther*, and *Star Wars*. It is thrilling for these young adults, many of whom were bullied as kids and suffered from low self-esteem. There is nothing more rewarding than this!

When I watch the daily news on TV, I am overwhelmed with the violence and cruelty in the world. But I get to see the other side in my everyday life. I see kindness and optimism. I am blessed to be part of a special-needs community determined to "repair the world."

My Recommendations

1. **Do not try to do this alone; it takes a village.** I don't really want to do anything alone. I want to have co-conspirators to brainstorm with and to console each other when things get tough. Two minds are generally better than one and three minds even better than that!

2. **Think outside of the box. Open the door to the possibilities.** Don't be afraid to try new things even if they seem outrageous to some. Do not listen to the naysayers. Be brave.

3. **Define your vision and mission. Beware of "mission creep."** It's easy to get off-target and stray from your mission in the excitement of the moment. Stay focused. It would be great if you could be everything to everyone. But you can't, so decide what is realistic. Developing a detailed strategic plan will allow you to put your dreams on paper.

4. **Be patient. Do not get discouraged.** It took Michelangelo four years to paint the ceiling of the Sistine Chapel. It took NASA eight years to put a man on the moon. Great ideas take time.

5. **Hire the brightest and best. They will make you look good.** Don't feel threatened by really smart people. You can't be an expert in everything. Talented people will bring innovative ideas and make your project successful. Be sure to credit their accomplishments and reward them appropriately.

6. **Be kind. Be your best self.** You need to set the example for everyone else.

My Wish for You

If you are reading this book, you already have "the right stuff." You know what you are passionate about and have at least a vague idea of what you want to accomplish. As you begin (or continue) your journey in the nonprofit world, stay true to your mission, believe in yourself, and don't be afraid to take the road less traveled. Margaret Mead is believed to have once said, "Never doubt that a small group of thoughtful, committed citizens can change the world. Indeed, it is the only thing that ever has." Gather your community, share your ideas, and take the plunge. You have the power to change the world!

My Community

Listen to my episode on the Xceptional Leaders podcast:

Mom Creates Autism Careers in
Digital Arts with Yudi Bennett

Ways to Connect with Me

Email:
yudibennett@foothillautism.org

Facebook:
https://www.facebook.com/yudi.b
ennett

Other Resources

www.foothillautism.org

www.exceptional-minds.org

www.uniquelyabledproject.org

Yudi Bennett is the co-founder of Exceptional Minds and Foothill Autism Alliance. She holds a master's degree in communications and a certificate from the LEND (Leadership Education in Neurodevelopmental Disabilities) Program. She has been a member of the Directors Guild of America for more than 40 years and received their Frank Capra Lifetime Achievement Award in 2003. She is also a member of the Academy of Motion Picture Arts & Sciences with credits in over 30 movies, including Broadcast News *and* Kramer vs. Kramer.

Leadership Embodied

Providing Education and Support for People with Disabilities in Nigeria

Celine Osukwu

I was born in Nigeria during a conflict. Months after my birth, my mother vacated her house for fear of bombing, which was so rampant there. We were internally displaced. We suffered hunger and starvation as the entire zone was cut off from access to milk, fish, salt, meat, and other essential foods. We were also cut off from medical facilities and drugs. So many women, children, and elderly people died of *kwashiorkor*, a form of malnutrition, and other complications. I became severely sick and passed out. I was taken to a makeshift hospital and was admitted and treated by a humanitarian agency which was giving relief services to women and children affected by the war. I survived but later became disabled.

Growing up was tough because I faced challenges from different sides. I am physically disabled by *kyphosis*, a condition that results in an abnormal curvature in the spine. Because of this, people told my mother to throw me away— they advised her to throw me in a pit or abandon me in a bush so I would die gradually. She refused all pieces of advice.

My life journey has been distorted by difficulties emanating from violence, discrimination, marginalization, and stigma as a person with a disability. At age ten I was denied a high school admission by the head teacher, notwithstanding my high score in the qualifying examination. She deemed me to be unqualified because I was a child with a disability.

As a result of this disability, I have been a target for ritual killers who sell human body parts. This is, unfortunately, a common thing in Nigeria, and people with disabilities are always at risk for physical harm. My mother was warned not to let me out of the house; however, at the age of 16, I went against her wishes because I was pursuing my desire for higher education and, fortunately, was divinely saved from the hands of a person who was known for ritually killing people with disabilities. Her mind has never been at rest since then, and to this day, she worries about me traveling.

In Nigeria, where I still live, apart from social stigmas associated with disability, persons with disabilities are seen as "good for nothing" and viewed as objects of charity. I live in an environment of social stratification based on gender and other status. I had difficulties going to school, not because I couldn't learn or walk to school but because of extreme poverty. In a family where people hardly get food to eat, schooling is a luxury, so a child with a disability is rarely educated. On several occasions, I went on hunger strikes, which was my way of expressing my disillusionment about the life I was subjected to live. The fact that my only surviving parent is helpless to change the system made my case so much more difficult.

I hardly have a constant job and can't even dream of securing a good-paying job in Nigeria. With poverty always lurking, I cannot afford a decent house as I live hand to mouth. Hunger is a driving force, which pushes disabled persons into the street begging. Unfortunately, Nigerian society prefers giving disabled persons on the streets money, rather than giving them paying jobs and shelter. The majority of people with disabilities see begging as the only sure source of income. However, as I mentioned earlier, begging exposes us to more physical danger. I have never begged in the streets.

As a woman living with a disability, I face double marginalization as I am discriminated against and marginalized on the basis of being a woman IN ADDITION to having a disability. Yet, I do not hold myself down because of these challenges.

In light of this, I am always subjected to severe constraints, living in poverty and struggling to attain some level of education. I have already earned both a bachelor's degree from the University of Benin, Benin City, Nigeria, and a master's from Middlesex University, London, UK, and hope to earn a doctoral degree in the future.

I have also had the blessing to travel, work, and learn. I was a steward to the World Council of Churches (WCC) Central Committee meeting in Geneva, Switzerland, (1999) and attended the international training institute of the World Young Women's Christian Association, (World YWCA, 2002). I have volunteered with the Parkinson's Disease Society of the United Kingdom (Enfield, London) and Amnesty International UK office, worked as an intern at the United Nations Department of Economic and Social Affairs, and participated in both the 9th Assembly of the WCC under the Ecumenical Disability Advocates Network, Porto Alegre, Brazil, and the tenth Assembly of the WCC, Busan, Korea.

In addition to traveling to Kenya (2007, 2017, 2019), Rwanda (2017), Togo (2015, 2016, 2017, 2019), Senegal (2007), and Ghana, I have also had international training on human rights in Indonesia (2010), Brazil (2011), and Germany (2017).

In 2011 and 2013, I met a good-spirited woman at a course, and she supported me for a trip to Canada for additional academic courses that boosted my skills and placed me in a better stead for work. I was able to study women's human rights at the University of Toronto and development leadership at St. Francis Xavier University, Canada. These courses empowered me with more skills that boosted my ability to deliver services related to development issues.

Unfortunately, even with advanced degrees and an extensive global education, I faced discrimination of all sorts. At workplaces, I was always relegated to the background and treated as if I were sub-human or as if I did not have rights equal to others'. My self-worth and integrity were always put to test. It became obvious to me that if I should go through these experiences, what about those who are less educated?

Often, I must inform others why I am motivated to create my offering focused toward a life of service for the less privileged, especially persons with disabilities. The challenges made me determined to assist others.

The journey to creation has been difficult at times, and I reached a peak of complete drain from June 2007 to Dec 2008. I was thoroughly exhausted. I had a target to support an average of 5,000 persons with disabilities in a year through training, sensitization, motivational speeches, writings, and direct financial support, but I was drained emotionally, physically, and economically.

During this time I had no job, lost my accommodation, and had no food to eat. I had no money to buy food, never mind provide support, food, or education for others. I seemed to have lost myself in supporting others. I was living with a family but was almost made a slave doing household chores and definitely lost focus on my bigger aspiration—empowering persons with disabilities.

As if this wasn't enough of a challenge, I also experienced discrimination and marginalization from a group of "women activists" who I thought I could lean on and draw strength from. This was the climax of my struggles. I felt used and dumped, treated like trash, and thrown away. I lost my self-worth. The little hope and emotional strength I gathered from my previous years of international experience seemed to have evaporated through agony and despondency.

I couldn't help but ask myself, "Is it really my fault that I am incapacitated for work demanding so much energy and resources? Am I really failing in my life goal of working for the improvement of life and better living standards of persons with disabilities? Maybe I bit off more than I can chew. Am I over-ambitious? How do I sustain myself while helping others when I need help myself?"

Unfortunately, I also experienced personal discrimination in the workplace, specifically related to administration. Although my colleagues pretended to be tolerant, when I brought up challenges related to my disability, they were not supportive and denied me their respect or acknowledgment. But I battled to regain my focus. The focus of trusting in the universe, trusting in God who breathed life into me, trusted in me and assuring myself that I can, yes I can. I recollected my internal strength and the things that uplifted me—things I had achieved for myself in the midst of the hardships I endured.

Since 2009, I have worked earnestly to surmount the plethora of barriers caused by exclusion, poverty, and discrimination. I am the Nigerian anchor person for the Ecumenical Disability Advocates Network, a program of the World Council of Churches, Geneva. I advocate for inclusive churches, knowing that all are made in the image of God. In addition, my privately established charity organization, Divine Foundation for Disabled Persons, helps persons with disabilities overcome poverty, gain a voice, acquire skills, live independent lives, and refrain from street begging. I formed and registered this charity organization in Nigeria, and through it, I work directly with persons with disabilities (PWDs) who are most vulnerable to poverty, hunger, abuse, violence, and disease. I train others in empowerment activities to help them live a life of integrity and self-worth because I believe that capacity building is of essence for self-confidence, as well as peace and well-being for PWDs. We do not want to live on charity and pity. PWDs need support to tackle unique challenges and lift ourselves up from societal stereotypes.

In my heart, I am very strong. I never allowed my physical disability to affect my goal of standing strong, especially in service to humanity. Supporting, empowering, and inspiring persons with disabilities and living a life of integrity and respect is my ultimate goal. I am mentally balanced. My sweet mother mentored me to appreciate my uniqueness. Her mantra to me is, "Use your mental ability to supplement your physical disability," and I so much cherish those words. I hold on to them.

My Inspiration

I was brought up in a rural community by an uneducated, widowed mother. The two of us have a strong attachment that is hard to break. I am her last child, the child

God gave to her in her middle years of life. I am the only child whom she saw pass through the "shadows of death" and come back to life. When she was most vulnerable, I developed a disability. She witnessed firsthand my ordeals and her ordeals, and the pains of her heart deepened her love for me. For me, she is an angel. She sees beauty in me. She sees me as a special gift from God and treats me as such. To her, I am that gift from which she will reap blessings in her old age. She appreciates the image of God in me and trusts me to help bring her a brighter future. Her sobbing voice was the only voice that I recognized while I was whiling away in an unknown world; that voice brought me back to life. She boldly identifies herself as my mother, regardless of the stigmatization she encounters.

She refused to write me off even when she was vulnerable herself. She champions my course as much as those of her other children, and she doesn't hesitate to rise in protecting and supporting me. She saw me pass through stages of discrimination and stigmatization. She was stigmatized alongside her disabled child. She became more resolute in her fight. My mother fought on different fronts to protect me.

My background and her strength have directed my goal to provide education and support to persons with disabilities, thereby empowering them to live a life of integrity, while advocating for their inclusion in societies. I do this because of my multiple experiences with marginalization and discrimination. Other persons with disabilities face similar things around the world. With a deep focus on my goal, strength, and determination to assist other helpless individuals, I have never been deterred or daunted by any limitation. I strongly believe that, in every situation, a hand of God is at work. The diversity of God daily reflects on everything in our world, yet we are equal before the Universe.

My Gifts

From creating my offering, I have personally grown. I have overcome emotions that initially held me down. I rose above my challenges and gained my voice; hence, I boldly speak on disability inclusion and advocate for recognition and consideration of the plights of persons with disabilities in policy issues. I have beaten stereotypes and still never give up the daily fight to attain more life goals and achieve dreams. I have gained writing and speaking skills through my engagements with national and international networks and partners. I also learn a lot from interacting with people while creating and growing my disability offering.

My spiritual growth has been tremendous. I have felt and recognized the hands of the universe in my life and have learned to lean on and trust more in God. I trust Him daily for my support, my help, and my protection from dangers, especially from the hands of ritual killers who target persons with my kind of disability. I walk boldly, talk boldly, and speak truth to power, knowing I am destined to serve others selflessly. My inclination to knowing God informed the name of my organization, Divine Foundation for Disabled Persons.

My financial growth has been slow, but it is still better than it was five years ago. In 2017, I was recognized as an impact leader by an online group, the World Pulse, as a result of my disability offering. The recognition came with a financial award that enabled me to reach out to more PWDs while keeping a paying job. With that support, I was able to save up a little money from my salary and continue serving others.

I continue to gain recognition and encouragement from others to create and grow my disability offering. In 2019, I was interviewed for the Xceptional Leaders podcast by Mai Ling Chan from the United States and for Feministo podcast, Episode 23, by Kirthi Jayakumar and Vaisnavi from India, as they learned of what I offer. The interviews were broadcast online and gave me publicity around the world.

My Recommendations

As a result of all of my experiences, ongoing education, and mentorship, I share these personal recommendations with you as you create and grow your disability-focused offering.

1. **Show love to yourself.** Self–love is very important and necessary for your growth. If you don't love and appreciate yourself, you cannot love others. It is only when you love others that you can render services to them. Be proud of who you are. Don't let your disability hold you down.

2. **Focus on your ability and not on your disability**. In other words, focus on your dreams and not on problems. If you focus on problems, the problems would magnify and overwhelm you, but if you focus on your dreams, inspiration comes in. Create visions for yourself, and continue to follow those visions.

3. **Trust in the Universe, and take responsibility**. There is no doubt that a Supreme Being is responsible for the things of this world. We put our trust in that Supreme

Being. Take responsibility; take charge of your offering. It is your calling, and you have to take it up by yourself to fulfill your calling.

My Wish for You

I have realized that I am not living with the most difficult challenges. Turning my challenges around, I have experienced the manifold joy and blessings that my offering brings. The same I pray for others—that they will graciously get closer to neighbors and to the realization that one's challenge is a trifle compared to that of others.

My Community

Listen to my episode on the Xceptional Leaders podcast

Empower Women with Disabilities with Celine Osukwu

Ways to Connect with Me

Facebook: @celine.osukwu

Celine Osukwu is an activist and passionate disability advocate whose activism encompasses many vulnerable groups. She has impacted thousands of grass-root Nigerian efforts through her development work activities and has empowered hundreds of persons with disabilities through direct support, training, research writings, and inspirational/motivational talks. Celine has not allowed

disability to stand in her way of serving others. She dedicates her life to serving humanity.

Opening Doors

Creating a Coffee Shop to Help her Son and Other People with Disabilities Flourish

Karin York

Photo by Chris York

The process of starting a new business was exhilarating. We went through all the motions of securing our name, designing our website, picking out colors, and decorating the shop. I pictured each adult with a disability—many my former students—and the perfect job each of them would have at the coffee shop.

The plans were drawn up, revised, and then submitted to the city for approval. This is where the process slowed. It took about three months of revisions for the city to finally approve our plans. However, we were still on a high; once plans were approved, we were ready to start making this dream a reality. Our general contractor indicated the build-out would be about three months; it was May, so I planned for an end of August opening. We rolled up our sleeves and got to work.

First up was plumbing. The plumbing quote was the first gut punch we received in the construction process. With a quote of more than $30,000, our savings account was almost wiped out, but we were determined to get the process started. Plumbing commenced, and with the sawing of concrete and digging of trenches, my dream was coming to life.

Sadly, as anyone who has done any renovation works knows, many problems began to arise. What started off as a ten-day project turned into a three-month ordeal, from battling dense concrete and soil to misreading of plans. They had to rip up all the plumbing and restructure the pipes due to this error.

Once the underground work was completed, we were ready for walls to go up. I quickly realized that, for construction to move along, I would have to wear the hat of general contractor. Getting trade workers to show up and do their part of the job was exhausting. I could not understand why jobs would be partially finished, and then days would go by before work would resume. We would enter the shop daily to check the progress only to be disappointed that the only work completed was from spiders making webs in the corners.

Eventually, walls went up, and we were ready for the electrician. Doing our due diligence, we received three quotes for electrical work. The expensive electrician cost and lengthy timeline were the final blows that made me question everything. I was consumed with overwhelming doubt and fear.

With the realization that we could not afford to continue, I contemplated returning to my teaching position. I broke down emotionally in my living room and told my husband that I wanted to go back to what I knew and trusted. Our finances were dwindling, and teaching produced a steady income. We both cried uncontrollably. We determined that we had given this endeavor everything—financially, physically, and emotionally. We truly had nothing more to give. Our crying was a hyperventilating, exhaustive kind of cry that is both cleansing yet draining. I forced some solace in knowing I had at the very least, tried. I pursued a dream, raised awareness, and sacrificed greatly.

But, something in me wouldn't let this project fade away. After my exhaustive cry, I found the strength to continue. I called a few friends, found additional funds, and made it through the very difficult inspection process.

Spencer's Place finally opened its doors in Surprise, Ariz., in February 2020. Our employees, most of whom are my former students, are so proud to have a job. Many stay at work after they have clocked out because they feel productive and purposeful. They are flourishing in positions such as greeter and cashier (with support), in addition to creative positions designing artwork and helping with new product names.

We all have a need to "fit in," but I believe this place celebrates our diversity.

My Inspiration

When I became the mother of a son with Down syndrome, my life was completely transformed. It was already rather chaotic with my current children, ages three and one, but this new little life meant I had to change. When Spencer was born in 1990, I was naive and, in some ways, ignorant. His disability didn't show any indications in utero; therefore, I was ill-prepared for his diagnosis. It was an instantaneous life-altering change. Technology was nonexistent, and the library was my only resource to gain information. I was introduced to a parent support group, and quite honestly, I did not find it helpful. Fortunately, my support system was strong and readily available within my family and church. I didn't know it at the time, but I was in a conditioning phase to become my son's advocate, as well as that of my future students.

Early intervention and six therapies per week drove me to a new level of discipline and controlled chaos. I was innately capable of so much more than I could have known. Because I already understood the muscle groups and functions, I felt driven to increase his muscle tone and motor skills. He miraculously hit many developmental milestones on time. I had several negative interactions with doctors and again, felt myself inching toward something unknown but empowering.

Several years later, I would find myself enrolled in college in pursuit of a physical education degree. At this time, Spencer was eight years old in a self-contained classroom and was continuing to learn the same material as he had every year: days of the week, months of the year, colors, weather, numbers, etc. He had mastered these skills, yet the daily ritual continued for hours without any extension or new developments. I visited my son's classroom often, concerned about his lack of academic growth. Yes, I was "that parent."

I called meetings with teachers and administrators weekly to voice my concerns. I was a bit neurotic and forceful, and they did not always appreciate my assistance. During my final encounter with my son's principal, he yelled the words I didn't know I needed to hear, "If you think you can do a better job, why don't you do it yourself!" I walked over to the front desk, withdrew Spencer from school, drove to Arizona State University and changed my major to special education. We finished out the school year with intensive learning at home.

The following school year, I found a school that was appropriate and shared my mindset. Spencer's educational goals were met, he was gaining social skills and transforming. While in college, I was invited to lead a reading group at his school. These leveled groups served as a training guide and showed me how to effectively differentiate instruction. I received a hands-on approach to this concept which would be my mantra in my future classroom.

I graduated from Arizona State University and began my special education career. I started off at the elementary level and incorporated many of my new strategies into the curriculum. As my students advanced into higher grades, I began to think about what the future would be for Spencer.

In 2006, Spencer entered high school; I was terrified at the realization that his transition to adulthood was nearing. I felt lost and began to investigate post high school options. I listed my hopes and dreams for him in a notebook. They were simple ideas jotted down to guide my thoughts. I had never heard of transition programs or day treatment programs for adults with disabilities. Researching was both time consuming and exhausting. I continued to develop my plans for his future, and they included a program that I would design. It was a grandiose establishment with a multifaceted approach. It had a fitness center, florist, cafe, bakery, coffee shop, and in-house photographer. Each of these professions would employ individuals with disabilities and offer a wide array of opportunities to develop workplace skills. I poured into this idea, located courses to guide me as a new business, began classes, and built my portfolio of dreams.

The following year, I was given an opportunity to open the self-contained special education program at a local high school. I had a new mission and gave it my everything. I transferred Spencer into my program and worked to meet the specific needs of my students. I was completely unaware of it at the time, but the design and implementation of this transition program was preparing me for Spencer's Place.

My students grew educationally and socially due to our comprehensive program. One of the most impactful memories that continues to inspire me is that of a 16-year-old student with intellectual or developmental disabilities (IDD). She could not read or identify all 26 letters of the alphabet. We piloted a new reading program and enforced it with fidelity. Within months, she was reading at the kindergarten level! She felt empowered and continued to work diligently to increase her reading level. By graduation, she had grown exponentially in both reading and writing. She is 25 years old now with a whole new lease on life. We remain in contact and meet monthly. Each time I receive a text message from her, I am reminded of the determination and unrelenting fortitude enlisted to make this simple text message happen. It opened the door for communication that would otherwise have remained untapped.

This example is one of many we experienced as we raised the bar and insisted on growth. Our program received awards and accolades for our test scores in each academic category. I found that, if I increased my expectations and provided leveled steps of instruction, my students could achieve anything! I modified the standard chemistry curriculum and taught three leveled courses with a lab. Some took notes via a scribe, some with a fill-in-the-blank accompanying worksheet and others directly from the slides. They flourished, and so did I.

The evidence of my students' potential drove me to continue raising the level of expectation. We studied literature,

Hemmingway, Steinbeck, Cisneros, and more. We acted out *12 Angry Men* and recognized new ways to inspire students. Administrators and staff visited our classroom often to witness the engagement and progress.

In addition to teaching, I took on a new position with an organization called "Capernaum." It is a division of Young Life International for individuals with disabilities. We meet several times a month for a fun-filled club activity or outing such as bowling. I contacted all my former students and their friends, and we met every other week for about two hours. To communicate with parents and members, I developed a group messaging system. Little did I know, this would be where I would learn of the mundane and unfulfilling details of some of my former students' lives. Each day I would read the messages that read, "Hello, everyone, how are you?" . . . "What are you doing?" . . . "Nothing" . . . "Playing video games". . . "Watching TV."

As we would approach the day of club, messages would start coming in like, "Who's going to club?". . . "Can't wait to see everyone" . . . "Best night of my week." Once that day came, kids would be outside waiting hours before club started. One girl started walking at 1 p.m. from Glendale to Surprise—about 20 miles—just to have some camaraderie with her former classmates.

The need to be accepted and valued was overwhelming. However, the desire to have a purpose in life was undeniable. Every day, the messages would start coming in and would be the same as the day before. I was haunted as I learned of the ongoing trials they faced to become employed. Many complained of sitting at home, losing skills, longing for a meaningful existence and needing something to fill the void in their lives. This was my breaking point where I knew I had to do something. The idea of opening a coffee shop was born.

My Gifts

My faith has been stretched and strengthened in ways I never knew possible. Through the unknown, I would prayerfully seek wisdom and guidance from God, and He never failed me. Through the disappointments, I believe He sent people that stood in the gap when I felt defeated. Through the financial strain on our family, strangers became friends and campaigned with their own fundraisers because they saw the desperate need for this coffee shop. I know none of this would have been possible without my trust in God. I would question sometimes whether He was in this and really leading me only to get confirmation soon afterward.

Personally, I have overcome limiting beliefs and getting outside my comfort zone. The fear of leaving my teaching career, something that was routine and reliable, initially prevented me from taking the risk. Familiarity is safe, but familiarity is not where we grow. Recognizing that I had this fear made me force myself to take on this risk. I would not let fear win. Support from my husband was key in tackling fear. He believed in me and my dream. When I wanted to give in, he would spur me on and remind me that fear is a liar. Our marriage has grown from the trials we faced during the planning and construction. When you are with someone who believes in you and is willing to stand with you or even go before you at times, it gives you the confidence to do the impossible. I am blessed to have Chris and his love and support to push me forward.

A strong support system celebrates miniscule milestones and raises awareness and funds. My friends, Daria and Valerie, spurred me daily, as did my mom and siblings. My sister, Erin, and niece, Alexandra, listened intently as I poured out my fears weekly. I found great support at my school and church and through my former athletes. Through social media I made new friends, such as Robert Thorton and Mai Ling Chan, who began fundraising campaigns as they chose to invest in this vision with us.

I feel empowered as the impact on the community has been tangible. It is like nothing I have experienced. People aren't just talking the talk, they are actively engaging in this idea. We embrace our differences and have discovered new ways they enhance our workplace daily!

My Recommendations

1. **Keep your dreams alive!** I became fully aware that if I didn't move forward, I would live with this looming regret. I had to embrace fear and the trepidation of leaving my teaching position, my safe place and steady income. With only six years remaining until my full retirement was vested, I battled the risky financial decision to step away and enter the unknown. I shared my dreams with people that would not only encourage me but would hold me accountable. They followed up with me, sent inspirational stories of similar concepts, and refused to let me fail. The support was ongoing and affirming. When I was in a state of despair, they reminded me of my mission. Choose wisely as your tribe will carry you.

2. **Ask for help**. Pull from every resource that you know and don't know, including social media. It is okay to be vulnerable and directly relay your specific needs. You will be surprised how many people will rally around you. I have discovered that there is so much goodness in this world, and people are truly there to help.

3. **Remember why you began this journey.** As I contemplated what seemed to be defeat I would constantly remind myself of the reason I started this venture. I would envision my future employees with disabilities and the inevitable anticipation of their first job.

4. **Set yourself up for success**. I spoke words of affirmation over myself and the coffee shop. I would even remind myself that all of this adversity has to be for a reason. If it was easy, it would not have the same value. I also followed several mentors that had taken great leaps of faith. One that resonates the most is Andrea Robinson, a news anchor who decided to leave her successful career to be at home with her children. Another is a fitness expert who fills me daily with powerful words and challenges.

My Wish for You

The phrase "get out of the boat" was my biggest push. This is in reference to Peter, one of Jesus' disciples, when he witnessed Jesus walking on water. Peter called out to Jesus and said, "Lord, if it's you, tell me to come to you on the water." Jesus told Peter to come. Peter got out of the boat and walked on the water.

It is fairly simple—to walk on water, you have to get out of the boat. We cannot walk on water if we are still clinging to the boat. There is a plan and vision for your life. If you want to do something greater than you can ever imagine, you have to have a big vision. You have to stand up, fix your eyes on that vision, swing one leg over the boat rail, get uncomfortable, steady yourself, have faith in your abilities, and swing the other leg over. Do not allow fear, worry, complacency, or the size of your vision distract you and cause you to lose focus. If something is planted in your heart and it haunts you day and night, you are called to take action. I read a meme that said "Making a life change is scary. You know what is even scarier? Regret." Keep your eyes fixed on your goal, let go of the side of the boat, and walk on water.

My Community

Listen to my episode on the Xceptional Leaders podcast:

Opening a Special Coffee Shop Part 1 with Karin York

Opening a Special Coffee Shop Part 2 with Karin York

Ways to Connect with Me

Website: www.spencersplaceaz.com
www.employedandoverjoyed.org

Facebook: Spencersplaceaz

Instagram: spencersplaceaz

Twitter: @PlaceAz

Visit us at: Spencer's Place

15341 W Waddell Road, Suite B101

Surprise, AZ 85379

Karin York is a parent of a son with a disability, a high school special education teacher, and an advocate. She recently stepped down from teaching to help her former students transition into the workforce by opening Spencer's Place, a coffee shop that employs adults with cognitive and developmental disabilities. Karin's passion for the marginalized drives her to inspire others to realize their full potential and worth within the community.

Part III: Embracing Tech

See a Need. Fill a Need.

Creating a Safe Minecraft Community for People with Autism

Stuart Duncan

Photo by Tyler Duncan

"See a need, fill a need" is the simple yet perfect advice that Bigweld gives for becoming a great inventor in the animated movie *Robots*. That phrase really struck a chord with me, and when my moment came, when I saw a need—against everything inside of me telling me not to—I took a chance and tried to fill that need.

In 2013, I saw parents of autistic children all over social media reaching out to other parents with posts basically saying the same thing: "Do you have a child with autism who likes Minecraft? Would they be willing to play with my child?"

I saw this question being asked more and more and discovered that it was because their children had a deep desire to play Minecraft with other people, make friends, and be a part of a community. Because having autism means behaving or reacting to situations differently than most other people, though, they became the targets of bullies and trolls everywhere they went. Parents discovered that their children couldn't fit in on any of those public servers, and they felt powerless to do anything about it.

Those bullies saw how angry autistic children got when they killed them, destroyed their builds, or stole their stuff, so they'd push it further and further to see how much of a reaction they could get. And if those bullies did discover that their victims were autistic, they'd say the most terrible things they could think of, such as, "Your parents never wanted a retard like you, so you should do them a favor and kill yourself."

It broke my heart to see this. I can't imagine what those children felt. All they wanted was to make a friend. To play. To be happy.

I saw a need. I decided to fill it.

My wife had just left me six months prior to this. I had no money and no extra time as I was already working 14-hour days, and I had no prior education or experience in setting up a Minecraft server, much less managing a community of autistic children. What I did have was a desire to help. I had to try.

In June 2013, I paid a hosting service for a Minecraft server and spent a few weeks making some buildings and a welcome sign and learning how to manage the plugins to keep players safe. Then, I opened the doors on June 23. That day, Autcraft, the first Minecraft server for children with autism, was born.

I shared my news about it on my private Facebook page—my friends list consisted of about 300 people at the time. To my surprise, I received more than 750 emails in the first 48 hours. I had no idea just how much of a need there really was for this.

Before making the announcement, I expected maybe one hundred players in total, if I was lucky. What I found was literally thousands of people filling my inbox within the first few months. I was paying a lot of money for hosting and spending a lot of time talking to people. My job performance suffered and I found myself running out of money a week before the end of each month. This turned out to be a much bigger challenge than I had ever anticipated.

I didn't have the money or the time, and I didn't know much about what I was doing but I stuck with it for one very important reason . . . the children. I talked to countless children who felt alone, scared, bullied, abused, or depressed and even some who were suicidal, and Autcraft gave them a home where they could be themselves and feel like they weren't alone anymore. On top of that, I heard stories about children making their first friends, learning how to read and write, getting their first jobs, graduating from high school, and so much more. I got emails from parents thanking me for making their children happy and even some letters thanking me for keeping their children alive.

I'm not going to lie to you. It wasn't an easy journey. I was working more than 120 hours a week for more than six years straight with no days off. Many of those days were extremely difficult, talking about depression, abuse, and even suicide with children who just couldn't take it anymore. I spent many 24-hour and even 36-hour long periods without sleep, helping people to survive just a little bit longer.

In fact, I have a confession to make. Writing this story has taken me months to complete. Why? Because as I write this, we are in the middle of the COVID-19 global pandemic. What this means to those of us on Autcraft is that we've been busier than we've ever been. In terms of numbers, we have more players playing than ever because, unlike summer vacation, kids are now home, unable to leave, and their parents are unable to go to work. Everyone is looking for ways to fill their days, for months on end. But it's not just the numbers—it's the fear, anxiety, depression, boredom, fatigue, anger, and so much more.

During one three–week stretch, I talked to children who lost their grandparents, one child who lost their favorite teacher to suicide, one of my admins who lost an uncle, and the list goes on. Children were out of their routine, and when autism is involved, routine is paramount to coping with the world on a daily basis. But routine didn't exist anymore. Children weren't going to school. They missed out on their proms and their graduation. They missed their friends, and understandably, they were angry that they didn't get a chance to say goodbye. The one thing they still had was Autcraft.

We tried to combat this by giving players more to do, such as events, parties, music concerts, mini-games, and a 75% off sale in the store (they buy stuff with points earned within the game), and we even changed up some default settings/rules on the server to make life a little easier to accommodate the larger number of players. All of this was our attempt to distract people from the world, to entertain, to keep people happy, to keep people busy . . . but ultimately, the hardest part was the talks. A lot of long, very exhausting, very heartbreaking talks.

Children had stopped eating, sleeping, taking care of themselves, doing the activities that keep them happy, and coping with stress. When this happens, they turn to the one place where they feel safe and accepted, Autcraft. But they go there already in a state of panic, anger, and stress. And we have to be there for them to help them through it. In a very real, unexpected sense, Autcraft became an "essential service" in the lives of literally thousands of families around the world. During the pandemic, I talked with dozens of children (and some adults) each day, about some of the most difficult things you could talk to a child about. I got about four hours of sleep each night, usually interrupted sleep.

It was not just me though. The people who volunteer their time to help me do this went through it too. They also put in their time, hearts, and souls for these children. During this time, the parents, the other adults, and even the children themselves were there for each other every single day because no matter how hard it is for us, we are always willing to do whatever we can to help make life better for you. And that is what Autcraft has become. Each of us uses our own struggles to give us strength and motivation to ease the suffering of other people because we don't want them to feel as bad as we do.

The entire world was quarantined in their own homes, a "lockdown" in which we were all separated to prevent the spread of this virus. But through Autcraft, a Minecraft server on the Internet, we all continued to be a community, a family, a support network . . . friends. We continued to be here for each other and support each other through life and through dark times.

My Gifts

I started Autcraft with one simple principle in mind: Every child deserves a safe place to play and have fun, free from fear.

The server has become so much more than that, but at its core, it is still just a Minecraft server where people can play Minecraft without worrying about bullies or trolls, a need that needed filling.

I see a lot of people trying to create something amazing and hoping that others will want it. That's one approach. But I find it's better to see what it is that people need, provide that, and let it become amazing.

I want to leave you with one final thought—not only do I have a son with autism, but I also have autism myself. When I tell people not to let your diagnosis hold you back, I speak from experience. I am an introvert, I am quiet, and I avoid talking to people at all costs, and yet here I am, creating one of the best communities on the Internet, consisting of over 12,000 people and climbing.

See a need, fill a need. It'll be the best thing you've ever done.

My Recommendations

These quotes have spoken to me the most and I have them plastered on signs in various places around the server for kids to find:

1. Never doubt that a small group of thoughtful, committed citizens can change the world. Indeed, it is the only thing that ever has. —attributed to Margaret Mead

2. *Sometimes it takes only one act of kindness and caring to change a person's life.* —attributed to Jackie Chan

3. *Do things for people, not because of who they are or what they can do in return, but because of who you are.* —attributed to Rabbi Harold S. Kushner

4. *You are braver than you believe, stronger than you seem, and smarter than you think.—* Christopher

Robin, *Pooh's Grand Adventure: The Search for Christopher Robin* (1997), often attributed to A. A. Milne

5. *In 900 years of time and space, and I've never met anybody who wasn't important before.* —Doctor Who (Matt Smith), *Doctor Who: A Christmas Carol* (2010)

The best teacher I ever had was my own mother, who told me once that she had made all of the mistakes in her life that I could ever make, but rather than prevent me from making those same mistakes, she'd just tell me how things worked out for her and then let me decide to do whatever I wanted to do from there. Maybe I'd do better, maybe I'd make the same mistakes, maybe I'd make new mistakes, but it was up to me.

My Wish For You

Stop trying to think of something amazing to do and then find people who will want it. Instead, find a need that people have, and fill it. Those people will find you, and it will be amazing. Don't wait. There will never be enough money, and it will never be the right time, but do it anyway. Figure it out as you go. It's worth it.

My Community

Listen to my episode on the Xceptional Leaders podcast:

Dad Makes Gaming Safe and Fun with Stuart Duncan

Ways to Connect with Me

Website: https://www.autcraft.com

Twitter: @autismfather

Instagram: @autismfather

Facebook: https://www.facebook.com/autismfather

Patreon: https://www.patreon.com/autismfather

Leveling Up

Accessibility in Gaming

Erin Hawley

Photo by Meinberg

It surprises people when I tell them I am confident and love myself. It surprises them even more when I tell them of my accomplishments, specifically the ones most people don't find "out of the ordinary" for the abled population, like graduating college or working. Of course, not every disabled person is able to do these things, and nothing is wrong with that. But my ability to do these ordinary things is nothing exceptional.

The challenge, for me, was always overcoming other people's expectations of what it meant to be disabled. The assumption, enforced through casual and overt ableism, as well as through capitalism, is that we have nothing to *give* to this world. Capitalism tells us if we aren't working, or if we receive any support needed to live in the community, we are a drain on society. It does not value friendship, emotional support, talents, love, and every other way we give as humans. To say we (disabled people) can't do any of those things is dehumanizing. But our existence is enough for us to matter.

Constantly having to prove your worth is tiring and degrading. But being able to defy expectations even when the bar is so low, and even when I shouldn't *have* to do that, builds up my love for myself. I am also lucky and privileged to have family and friends for support, who always, intrinsically, understood my value in this world and gave me the tools needed to pursue my goals. Not everyone has those supports, and through advocacy, writing, and community, it's something I try to give to others.

My Inspiration

One of my many hobbies is video gaming. Growing up, I played both PC and console gaming, starting with the Atari and a Commodore 64, and working my way up to PlayStation and streaming games on my computer. Console gaming in particular is nostalgic; some of my best memories center around sitting on the carpet of our neighbor's living room floor, playing on a Super Nintendo with my brother and our family friends. At the time, gaming was a style of play that was really accessible. I was matched equally in skill with my abled friends and family—and at my best in racing games—and I held my own in more difficult games like Mortal Combat and Super Mario, too.

As my muscular dystrophy progressed in the '90s and early aughts, and as game controllers became more complex, I found myself unable to play most games on a console. Most 1980s controllers started out with two buttons, but this grew to ten or more on modern systems like PlayStation and Xbox. Not only was I cut off from a hobby I adored, but I also felt like I was missing out on culture itself. Of course, I still had access to art, the Internet, and other cultural phenomena, but gaming was huge in my house and in my community. I could watch my brother play and share in the experience that way, but I, of course, wanted to try a game for myself and become immersed in that virtual world. My college dorm mates had game night in the common room, but again, I could only watch and cheer on. At the time, it didn't feel like that big of a deal because it was my new normal. I understood and accepted the limitations of my disability (I always have), so I assumed that was it—I was relegated to always watching but never partaking in console gaming again.

In the 2010s, I turned back to PC gaming after meeting other disabled people online. Until that point, I had only ever played on PC in the '80s and '90s, and a few free games on my Mac. In my mind at the time, the best games, and the ones I was most interested in, were on a console, which I could no longer access, so I tried to tune out most gaming news and hype. But by chatting with other disabled people online, I discovered that PC gaming was still a big thing, and, depending on who you ask, better than console gaming. PC gaming is more accessible and customizable. Instead of being locked into one input, you could use different types of keyboards, mice, and software to make games on a computer work for someone with a physical disability. Because I could already navigate a keyboard and mouse with relative ease, gaming with these tools was an obvious win.

But I was still met with challenges in this hobby. Many games, no matter my use of a keyboard or mouse, were still inaccessible completely or difficult to play. Button remapping, which lets you reassign the space bar, for instance, with a mouse button, was missing from a lot of games; when you can't reach certain keys, the lack of this feature is frustrating. Other accessibility fails include having to hold down more than one key at a time, having to press a button repeatedly in quick succession, lack of subtitles, and more. So even though PC gaming was more accessible than console gaming, it wasn't and still isn't perfect.

I wanted to do something about that.

My Gifts

In 2006, I graduated with a BA in English literature. With all that education behind me, I became an experienced and much-improved writer. In 2013, I took that skill, combined it with my love of all things nerdy, and started a blog called The Geeky Gimp. I chose that name because I wanted to take a word that is often used as a slur and turn it into something powerful. My goal with the blog was to share with abled and disabled people my obsessions, and to promote inclusive media through my posts. I didn't just write about video games—I wrote about board game accessibility, disability representation on *Star Trek* and other TV shows, disabled people in comic books, and other relevant topics. I also brought on other disabled writers to share their experiences.

This blog was the best decision I've ever made because it connected me with brilliant, creative, and passionate people who also wanted accessibility and inclusivity in their media. A few of the posts have gone viral, and I am extremely proud of the work I did and continue to do under The Geeky Gimp moniker. When I first started the blog, I did not expect the reception it's received, nor the connections I've made through it. And one of those connections was with Microsoft.

In 2016, Bryce Johnson—Inclusive Lead, Microsoft Devices, Xbox Adaptive Controller—contacted me about making console gaming more accessible for me. He found me through my blog and Twitter, and we chatted on the phone about my options. Fast forward another year, and Bryce told me about a controller Xbox was working on and was wondering if I would be interested in play-testing it. After signing a non-disclosure agreement, Bryce sent me (and other disabled gamers) the prototype. Back in the testing stages, we had to use a secret name, but when it was finally released to the public, it was called the Xbox Adaptive Controller.

The Xbox Adaptive Controller, quite literally, is a game changer. Through the various ports and variable setup options, this product opened up console gaming once again for me and invited in disabled people who were never able to game before, whether on PC or Xbox. The controller works for both platforms, and is sold at a reasonable price compared to other accessible buttons. This was the first time a major game company put in so much effort to develop and sell such a controller, and its reception was dynamite. An ad played for it even played during the Super Bowl.

A few months before it was released, I was invited to Jersey City, New Jersey, to film the launch video for the Xbox Adaptive Controller. Public speaking has always been my weak spot; whenever I have to say something, even if I plan it out perfectly in my head, my mind goes blank when the spotlight turns on. That video was the first time I've ever done a professional shoot, so I was nervous that I would mess it up. But I did it through sheer will, and it led me to be even more confident in my public speaking. It also helps that the video has over two million views.

Bryce, the product lead, said I was one of the inspirations for designing the Xbox Adaptive Controller, and that makes the work I do as The Geeky Gimp important. It means that my push for inclusivity is making a difference. Since my experience with Xbox and Microsoft, I have gone on to playtest other games and gaming devices for major companies like Logitech, Electronic Arts, Adobe, and others. I was featured in publications like *The New York Times*, *USA Today*, and the *Asbury Park Press*. I've also spoken on panels at conventions, with my most notable being at the 2018 Games For Change Festival at Parsons School of Design in NYC. That panel was even more nerve-wracking than the launch video because I wasn't just talking to a camera; everyone in the room had their eyes on me, but I didn't waver in my words.

Of course, I did not stop blogging. Recently, I branched out into vlogging—sharing my life on YouTube. I am still getting used to being on camera, but the more I do it, the better and more comfortable I will become. I am still figuring out a schedule that works best for me as far as shooting and editing videos because I rely on my family to set up and film with my cameras—I can't hold them up on my own. But sharing my view of the world this way is important. I don't just want people to read my words; I want them to see and/or hear me. Disabled people in video-related media, whether it's on TV, in the movies, or on YouTube, are underrepresented, so making this vlog series has been incredibly rewarding and fulfilling. I've met other disabled vloggers who both inspire me to keep producing content and amaze me in their talents as well.

My Recommendations

1. **Hire/consult with disabled people.** If you are not disabled yourself, ensure what you are doing is as inclusive and realistic as possible. The population you want to serve knows best about their needs. You might

also receive some suggestions that improve your work immensely.

2. **Find inspiration.** Look to other disabled people for inspiration. One person's experience is just that: one person's. It's important to be as diverse as possible within the disability community.

3. **Set realistic goals and expectations.** If you want to write a book, for example, don't say you want to write one chapter a day when you are working full time. If you want to stream video games, don't think you will gain a million followers in a year. Work small and celebrate those small victories.

4. **Be kind to yourself.** If you don't meet your goal, try not to beat yourself up. These are not always failures, as you can always learn and grow from your missteps. I have a Ph.D. in spinning the negative into the positive, and it's worked pretty well for me.

My Wish for You

I hope you are able to make a difference too, no matter what you are pursuing. In my experience, pushing past any doubts or fears I had about my work was critical to its success. If I didn't start my blog, I would not have met Bryce or done any of the aforementioned work. It's also important to realize that it's okay to be scared, and it's okay to be anxious. These feelings are a part of who we are too, and getting over those emotions to leap into a new endeavor can feel daunting. But when you feel like you can't do it on your own, reach out to others doing what you want to do—you will be surprised how many of them will know exactly what you are going through.

Know that I have failed many, many times, but I can't use those failures as a reason not to pursue my dreams; if I did, I would get nothing done.

My Community

Listen to my episode on the Xceptional Leaders podcast:

Adaptive Gaming with Erin Hawley

Ways to Connect with Me

Twitter:@geekygimp

Instagram: @thegeekygimp

Website:
https://www.geekygimp.com

Twitch: https://www.twitch.tv/geekygimp

YouTube: https://www.youtube.com/user/thegeekygimp

Erin Hawley is an accessibility consultant for video and board games. She also creates digital content focused on all things geeky and has appeared in The New York Times, USA Today, *Microsoft's Xbox Adaptive Controller launch video, and more.*

Random fun fact: Erin is also from Mai Ling's hometown, Keyport, New Jersey.

World Changers

Envisioning, Creating, and Leading an Accessible Life

Martyn Sibley

Photo by Hugh O'Neill

You read about entrepreneurs running out of money and facing the fear that their big dream is over all the time. It very often feels like a cliché or something in a riveting movie. However, on that cold December day in London, this was my reality.

I had quit my secure job barely six months before. It had all gone so well, too. After two years of getting great feedback on my blog and requests to work with me on a freelance basis, I felt the time was right to go solo. In some ways, the day I handed in my notice was a little impulsive. On the other hand, I said that I would be working for a good ten weeks longer so they could find my replacement and so I could get everything in order for this new chapter.

I had some anxiety, but really I was very excited. I was finally going to live the entrepreneurial dream. I immediately set about lining up a few consultancy contracts and preparing my website and marketing materials. My first day of self-employment was July 4, 2011. Even as a British guy, the fact this was Independence Day was not lost on me.

"So how could the dream be in such despair only a few months later?" I hear you ask. Well after the first few contracts, where I was paid to run webinars, the model was less in demand. Whilst I was speaking to some good leads and pivoting on the services I could offer them, my bank balance was running very, very low.

So many thoughts crossed my mind. I wouldn't be able to afford the cost of my accessible flat, which had taken so long to find when I first moved to London. What would my family think about me quitting so soon? Furthermore, what about all of the people I was planning to impact? I felt like I was letting them down, too. My mind was racing, I felt sick, shivering with the icy weather, and I questioned everything about my path.

It would have been so easy to just look for a similar job to the one I had previously. The pay and the holidays were not so bad either. Yet, the dream still pulled me forward and wouldn't allow me to throw in the towel. So in that crunch moment, looking out my window, I started to think outside the box, planning for any way to get me through this dark moment.

During that difficult spell, somewhat of a crossroads you might say, my dream kept me going. Now, after lots of failures and some successes, I know that my dream is for a fully inclusive world. It wasn't always so simple to articulate, but on different levels, it was always there, spurring me on.

Having my genetic impairment since birth means that the barriers in everyday life have impacted me for a long time. I was born with spinal muscular atrophy type 2. The science part says that my body doesn't produce a particular protein that is vital for the brain's messages to reach and stimulate the muscles. Practically, I have always needed a lot of support for everyday tasks and a lot of equipment like my wheelchair, hoist, and adapted vehicle, to get around.

As I mentioned before, I believe that I am "disabled" by the barriers in society, which are categorized under the physical environment, people's attitudes, and organizational policies. I was taught this during my job at the disability charity

Scope. Like many other disabled people before me, this was a very liberating model to discover.

Here is an example of each type of barrier:

- If a building has steps, I am disabled. However, when a building has ramps or elevators, I am Martyn.

- If I meet someone in the street and they presume I am unable to speak or think for myself because I'm in a wheelchair, I am disabled. If that person treats me at face value and is curious to get to know me as a person, I am Martyn.

- If I go for a job interview and the employer doesn't allow flexible or home working, I am disabled. If an employer identifies my talent and potential and is willing to be flexible with how the job is done, I am Martyn.

The social model states how society can design for inclusion, rather than only looking for a medical cure. This doesn't mean that medical intervention is ignored, but rather disabled people are valued members of society, regardless of our physical limitations.

My Inspiration

One such medical intervention that was important for my life was the spinal fusion surgery that I had in 1999. It was the year before my exams at school. I had gradually been getting more hunched over due to the scoliosis of my spine. Despite body braces, which were not particularly comfortable, the surgery was the only way to ensure my breathing and sitting posture would be better for a fulfilled life.

Weirdly, it was after the operation that I really got to dreaming big. I was lying on my back looking up at the hospital ceiling in pain and also bored. I started to dream about all of the places I would visit in the world, all of the crazy adventures I would have, and all the people I would encourage to be their best selves.

After a long recovery, including anxiety attacks and losing a lot of bodyweight, I passed my exams. I then took the leap to go to university and have care support from people other than my parents. There, I learned economics, earned a master's in marketing, discovered how to drink until late into the night, and learned other things that are best left out of this book. From here, I had the confidence to travel to Australia for my first independent holiday. Then I got my job at Scope.

When I mentioned my blog earlier, this was the time when I was able to use my travels and adventures to help impact other people. Having spoken to a group of teenagers with the same disability as me, I wanted to spread this inspiring message further. The blog was my tool, along with social media. My message was that everything is possible when you believe.

I managed to overcome that horrible lull in finances in December 2011 by living in Spain on a fully funded project for three months, and renting my London flat out on Airbnb. Skills! I was then able to find solutions to my freelance offering, grow *Disability Horizons* magazine, launch Accomable (which was eventually exited to Airbnb in 2017), and head off on so many more global travels and adventures. Including scuba diving, flying a plane, husky dog sledding, and hot air ballooning. The stories are on my website and were featured in other media outlets.

My Gifts

Through all of my projects, businesses, and life experiences, I have seen both altruistic benefits and personal benefits. When I was growing up with my disability, I just wanted everyday life to be simpler. Even now in my mid-30s, I see so many barriers that do not need to be there. My dream of a fully inclusive world naturally will benefit me; however, as I have grown older and met people with a disability similar to mine, this dream created a fire in my belly to share my life experiences to help them uncover their path. This was the fuel that propelled me to spend hours upon hours on my blog in 2009 and to quit my comfortable day job in 2011.

As you can imagine, the lull of December 2011 wasn't the only dip in my journey. During the time of the accessible accommodation start-up business Accomable, I struggled for energy and health. From this mini-burnout, I went on a personal development journey, to find out how to change the world and still be happy and healthy.

In more recent years, I have grown the invisible muscle of compassion. I now understand better how it is to live with other disabilities, like having a visual impairment, hearing impairment, or being neurodiverse. Moreover, I can see that inclusion doesn't just mean with disabled people. The attitudinal barriers that we discussed earlier in this chapter apply to other marginalized groups. So to overcome all attitudinal barriers will include people from many other walks of life than disability.

I still want to achieve many more things for inclusion. Funding is a common thread of limitation. I am grateful that I have earned enough money to be self-employed sustainably for more than eight years now. Plus, the free travels were a massive bonus! So I want to acknowledge the income I have made but also would like more of an abundance of it to make a greater impact in the world.

My Recommendations

As a result of all of my experiences, ongoing education, and mentorship, I share these personal recommendations with you as you create and grow your disability-focused offering:

1. **Try to uncover your dream and path.** This doesn't mean getting frustrated when it doesn't appear quickly or obviously, but do give yourself the space to become aware of your passions. For example, I find journaling and walking the dog very useful in finding my clarity.

2. **Plan the next steps.** Once you have that big fluffy vision to aim for, to get you out of bed every morning and propel you forward for the long game, take the time to plan the next steps. I believe that it's worth aiming for the stars because even if we land on the moon, it's amazing. However, even getting to the moon takes a lot of preparation! So get in good practice of listing the things to do today or this week that move you even one step forward.

3. **Look after number one.** When I was in my twenties I was able to wake up early, go to work, do my side hustle, go partying, and eat pretty bad food. During my mini-burnout, I was in my early 30s, and my big

realization was that I have to look after my mind and body more. Particularly because I want to create an impact for many more decades to come. So find out what good health means to you, and create new habits to nurture that. My life is a little different now than ten years ago, but I took those improvements in small steps. Most of all, I still have a lot of joy from my diet and my daily routine, so don't let health become synonymous with pain and misery.

4. **Always learn, and grow.** One of the biggest mistakes I made was to think I knew everything. It's only been since I became more curious and admitted how little I truly know that my business has grown. So consume interesting blogs, books, and podcasts from your virtual mentors. Also seek out real-life mentors. It's surprising how easily done this is when you think about what support you need and just ask relevant people. Most of all, look to partner and collaborate because you will teach and learn in equal measures.

5. **Most of all, have fun!** It's easy to get bogged down in all of the serious business stuff, and the negative social issues in the world. So celebrate your wins, acknowledge how far you've come, and enjoy some rich leisure experiences. After all, too much work makes Jack a dull boy.

My Wish for You

I hope my story and thoughts are helpful to you. Most of all, my wish for you is to find something in the world that you truly care about, to uncover a cause that gives you true purpose and passion. In finding this rocket fuel and channeling it with a plan, I know that you will change the world so much.

Whilst making important change, I also hope that you look after yourself and enjoy the everyday smaller things in life. Do not let your mission overtake the human experience. Finally, which flies in the face of historical social narratives, I hope you enjoy wild success as an entrepreneur, and make an abundance of money.

From my experience, you really can have your cake and eat it!

My Community

Listen to my episode on the Xceptional Leaders podcast:

Everything is Possible with Martyn Sibley

Ways to Connect with Me

Websites:

World Changers Academy

https://xceptionaled.com/martyn-sibley-vip-academy-2/

My blog

www.martynsibley.com

Disability Horizons community

www.disabilityhorizons.com

Twitter: @martynsibley

Instagram: @martynsibley

Facebook: https://m.facebook.com/martynsibleyblog/

LinkedIn: https://www.linkedin.com/in/martyn-sibley-1227b411/

Part IV: Beyond the Label

What Life is Really Like

Capturing and Sharing Daily Disability Challenges through Award-Winning Shows

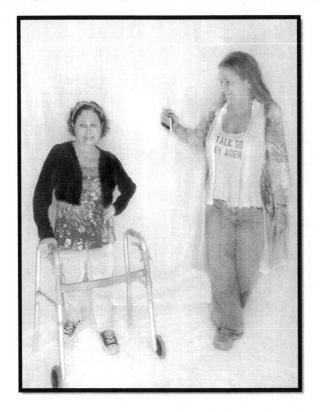

Peggy Lane

Left to right: Donna Russo and Peggy Lane; Photo by
Suzanne Allison

I began my professional career as a child model at age five in Chicago. I won substantial modeling work early on, and this led to acting opportunities.

When my father retired, we moved to California. That's when I started getting work in TV and films. I had a recurring role as a waitress on the comedy show *Seinfeld* and appeared on the shows *King of Queens* and *Will & Grace*.

I saw on some shows how the actors weren't part of the creation of the show, and wanting more involvement, I was inspired to write and produce my own shows.

My Inspiration

The inspiration for my *Donna On The Go* show is my friend, Donna Russo. She is a professional dancer and actress who now uses a walker or wheelchair to get around. She is also my roommate.

Our story began after my mother passed away in 2008, and my father's health began to decline. It's like he kept himself well for her, and once my mother passed, he felt his job was over. I knew I couldn't give him his health, but I could do the next best thing: I could give him something to look forward to.

I encouraged him to take small trips, like the one to Las Vegas where we saw a man on a scooter with oxygen attached to it. My dad said that was "sad." I disagreed. I maintained that he was out and about no matter what. "Who cares what people think? Despite all that man's challenges, he got out of the house and went somewhere he wanted to go. That's the opposite of sad. Sad would be not going out at all."

I encouraged and supported my dad as he attended three of his WWII reunions (103rd Army Cactus Division) and then eventually visited Hawaii and Ireland.

Around that time, I also moved into a two-bedroom, two-bathroom apartment so my dad could stay with me. After my father passed away in 2014, I went through a series of roommates. Some were better than others, and then I met Donna.

Donna told me she was diagnosed with Turner Syndrome (short stature, missing X chromosome, failure of the ovaries to develop, and heart defects) and Facioscapulohumeral muscular dystrophy (FSH MD), where the muscles of the face, shoulder blades, and upper arms are most affected). She had also broken her hip. It was a trifecta of challenges.

It's hard to find an accessible apartment. I knew that from looking for a place for my dad. My apartment in Burbank, Calif., has an elevator, NO stairs, and a wheelchair ramp out front, and the apartment is on the first floor. The only thing missing for the second bedroom was an accessible shower. After meeting and interviewing Donna, I offered to let her use my shower stall, figuring that the shower tub would be too hard for her to get in and out of.

That did it. She accepted my offer and pulled out her checkbook, and I had a new roommate. During our early days together of getting to know each other, I watched her slowly but surely go to her wheelchair dancing classes, and I thought that was awesome. Here I was, able-bodied but tired after work, and there she was, with all sorts of challenges doing something creative. I saw how everything she did was at least 10 to 100 times harder for her to do, but she did it anyway. That inspired me, and I knew it could inspire others as well.

One day, I saw her going out oh-so-slowly, and I teased her by calling her "Donna On The Go." She laughed. It stuck.

I had experience with walkers and wheelchairs from helping both of my parents. At one point, they were both using walkers and wheelchairs, and I almost had a breakdown. Fortunately, that phase didn't last long, and my dad was able to walk without one for a while. But whew, was that a challenge for both of us!

I've also witnessed Donna using walkers and fall a few times. Because I had learned from my parents' nurses, I knew how to properly lift her, assist her in and out of bed, and help her on and off the toilet. She fell pretty hard in 2018 on the day before the Emmys®. We had tickets but couldn't go. Instead we ordered in from IHOP and watched them on TV.

So what sparked the idea of *Donna On The Go*, the show? One day, Donna and I were shopping in Target, and she was trying to use one of the store's motorized scooters to go up and down the aisles. Since she's so small, she couldn't sit all the way back on the seat, and the scooter didn't seem to know she was on it. The scooter sputtered into "STOP" and "GO" jerkiness each time she tried to control it. We laughed so hard, we cried.

That's when I decided to film her on my iPhone. I wanted to make her laugh when she re-watched the clip later.

I had the idea to film her as she came around the corner, drove up an aisle and reached for something on the top shelf way out of her reach. From working with camera crews on the set of big-name TV shows, I knew it would take about an hour to set up and light a dolly tracking shot like that. You have to lay down an actual dolly track, which looks something like a small railroad track, and light it just right for every angle being filmed.

Instead, I tested the shot I had in my head with my iPhone, and guess what, it worked! I had managed to do something akin to a major camera set up in less than a minute, and it looked really funny! With that first shot, a show was born, and Donna has been as much of a blessing and friend to me as I hope I've been to her.

My biggest challenge was and continues to be financial. To create a show and get it produced requires fundraising, which is never easy. It's hard to ask for money—at least it is for me. It's also not always a creative thing to spend energy on, but it is the very first step in creating a show.

My big moment came in December 2016 when the Television Academy (they produce the Emmy awards) added a brand new category. They called it "Short Form," and it was designed for programs shorter than traditional network shows. These shows could have a running time of 15 minutes and under.

Still worried about potential financial constraints, I kept an eye on the category to see how it played out. Surprisingly, one of the shows nominated for an Emmy in this category was released on YouTube, and another show was hosted on its own website. Some show nominees were supported on larger cable channels, such as Comedy Central, but several successful shows required less financial overhead. This proved to me that *Donna On The Go* had an opportunity in this category. It was a chance, and all I needed was a chance.

After 18 years of being in the Television Academy, this was the first time I might have a shot to produce my own show. The day after the 2016 Emmy awards aired, I organized a production team, including director Craig Hutchison, a producing partner from New Zealand and a Godsend; Donna Russo, our lead actress; a writer; and me. We put together an outline and made a plan based on target dates.

There was so much to do. We had to write the script, find a cast, scout locations, plan the budget, raise money and apply for filming permits. Additionally, the Screen Actors Guild - American Federation of Television and Radio Artists (SAG-AFTRA) union paperwork must be completed for each and every actor, and they require proof of insurance and all the aforementioned before they will grant you clearance to film. Then you have to film it, edit it, and promote it.

Of course, there are also the Emmy target dates to keep in mind. Events called "For Your Consideration" (for Emmy hopefuls) start up as early as February, so everything had to be done before then. It wasn't.

As good as the first scripts were (and they were really, really good), they just weren't completed in time to get everything done so we could to compete. But that didn't stop me. I was NOT going to miss this opportunity. I couldn't. I knew year after year this category would get more and more famous people involved, and someone like me, without a major network or a powerhouse agent, wouldn't stand a chance. So our team had a talk, and we agreed to put our show together in less than two months. Ultimately, we did it.

In 2017, *Donna On The Go* (YouTube) appeared on the Emmy pre-ballot. The pre-ballot is a list of about 50 shows that qualified—met all the rules—of the Academy. People vote for these, and the top five go on to be officially nominated. *Donna On The Go* also appeared on the Emmy pre-ballot in 2018 and was submitted for consideration in 2019.

As of February 2020, the show has won 50 film industry awards internationally and has been submitted to more than 200 film festivals worldwide. People in Africa, Australia, Austria, Finland, France, Germany, Greece, India, Ireland, Italy, New Zealand, Norway, Poland, Romania, Russia, Scotland, Spain, Sweden, and the UK have watched the show. The show recently won a prestigious Telly Award and was nominated for an Indie Series Award for actress Kate Linder.

I did it! Something I filmed on my iPhone and shot around my own apartment complex is being seen and loved by people all over the world. It still blows me away.

My Gifts

Since creating *Donna On The Go,* I have had the gift of achieving all the creative things I wanted to do without the luxury of having a lot of time to do them.

Because we had to put the show together quickly, I wrote the show (six episodes to qualify for Emmy consideration); filmed it myself on an iPhone (no time to wait for rendering or to wait for someone to get back to me when they had time); directed all six episodes; edited them, and then personally promoted the show.

I used 25+ years of contacts within the television industry and let them know about the show. I bought ads on Facebook and made my own posters. I created a *Donna On The Go* website and housed the episodes there. I booked interviews, and Donna contacted her radio friends. I couldn't afford a publicist ($3,000–$5,000 in award season), so I became one.

About a month after promoting it, I ran into a colleague at an Emmy event. He looked at Donna and said "Donna On The Go!" I was THRILLED! I had built a little brand in less than a month that people recognized. I did that!

If I could do that, what else could I do?

Well it turned out, I could also inspire people. Many people have written to us or have told us that they were moved to tears by the show, Donna's dancing, and her sense of humor. Donna is now an Ambassador for the Abilities Expo Los Angeles, and for the last three years, we have had a booth there promoting the show.

Last year, a woman came by our Abilities Expo booth in a bed-like wheelchair utilizing an augmentative and alternative communication device. While at our booth, she watched "Donna On The Go: STAIRS," which features Donna walking up to a set of stairs that look "like a mountain" to her and then looking far away at the handicapped ramp meant to help her. In this episode, Donna begins the long walk to the ramp, complete with a time counter to the strains of The Pink Panther. The woman watched the show for a while and then, using her device, communicated, "That's me."

It was all I could do to not cry at hearing what she said, knowing full well how hard it was for her to say it. But I also thought, "Where else can she see herself?" There isn't much representation in film and television for people with disabilities. Often when there is a role for a person with a handicap, it goes to an able-bodied actor. For example, in the sitcom *Mom*, the actor in the wheelchair is an able-bodied actor, as is the actor in the sitcom *Superstore*.

There's no show like this with a LEAD character with a disability (not a funny friend, but THE lead) who entertains and enlightens in a humorous way. As I learned from being on *Will & Grace* for seven years, I know how laughter can be a gentle teacher. That has always been my goal for the show.

My Recommendations

1. **Tell YOUR story**. No one has a story like yours. Almost everyone has a smartphone. Use it. Create something. Film yourself and your friends, either talk to the camera, or write a little story. Inform people, and teach them empathy for others. Go out in the world and film things that inconvenience you. A doctor's office, a handicapped spot by a set of stairs, or a sidewalk that can't be rolled over are all perfect settings. This is how change happens. Put your story out, share it, and start being the change you want to see in the world.

2. **Give yourself permission to learn.** Try something, and let go of the worry around being perfect. It's okay if your ambitions exceed your ability. That's how you progress. Keep practicing, and you will grow as an artist. What do you have to lose?

3. **Find other like-minded people**. Maybe you have a friend with an iPhone who likes to shoot video? Maybe you're the one who likes to film things? Find one other person who believes in you and likes your idea, and you're on your way!

My Wish for You

Success only comes to those willing to fail.

My wish for you is that you find your passion. Whether it's being able to make people laugh at absurdity or shining a harsh light on inequities or a combination of both, finding your passion is the one thing that will fuel you. Finding your voice will emerge from that.

I also wish that your passions bring you joy. Besides *Donna On The Go,* which has fueled my daily passion for the last three years, I love dogs. My dogs have rescued me and bring me great happiness. One of them, Remington, was with me during the last few weeks of my father's life. I never would have gotten through that overwhelming sadness without that joy in my life. Another dog, Max, has adopted Donna. One day I was leaving for work, and I told him to keep an eye on Donna and make sure that the other dogs didn't knock her over (she's 4' 5" and about 90 lbs). When I came home from work, Donna said, "He's been following me around all day!" He had never done that before.

So I incorporated both passions—Max became an ambassador for the Abilities Expo Los Angeles and is featured with Donna in a promo and also on the show.

Mix your passions, and let them support each other.

Lastly, I wish you all the luck and courage in the world. You can make a difference. Everyone can.

My Community

Listen to my episode on the Xceptional Leaders podcast:

Writing and Producing Disability Focused TV Shows with Peggy Lane

Ways to Connect with Me

Website: https://www.donna-on-the-go.com/

Facebook: https://www.facebook.com/DonnaOnTheGo/

YouTube: Donna On the Go

Instagram: @peggylane1120

Real Life. Real People.

Going Behind the Camera to Share the Stories of People who Stutter

John Gomez

MA, CCC-SLP

Photo by Michaelan George

So, how in the hell did I ever think to make a documentary about stuttering? I am not a person who stutters, and technically, I am not, or at least I was not, a filmmaker. The idea for *WHEN I STUTTER* came to me when I was a student trying to get through a famously competitive communication disorders program at California State University, Los Angeles (Cal State, LA). It is probably also worth mentioning that prior to the summer of 2008, my level of interest in stuttering was no greater than in any other communication disorder. That changed when I met Gail Wilson Lew. Without her, *WHEN I STUTTER* probably wouldn't exist.

To refer to graduate school as "challenging" is an oversimplification. The process one goes through to become a speech-language pathologist is reminiscent of the old Winston Churchill saying, "If you are going through hell, keep going." To further complicate matters, I did the one thing that the department vehemently recommended against—I worked. Out of financial necessity, I maintained my job as a hotel valet and as a wedding videographer. Because of the chaotic nature of my life, I made up my mind that "getting by" was going to have to be enough. Survival was the name of the game.

In the summer of 2008 I took a life-changing stuttering course. By sheer happenstance, there had been a change in instructors. The graduate-level class was normally taught by the prolific Dr. Cari Flint. She is a woman of incredible teaching talent and had also been the instructor for the undergraduate stuttering course. That course was instrumental in teaching me some of the research and basic science behind stuttering. Due to her overwhelming schedule that summer, Dr. Flint invited Gail Wilson Lew to teach the graduate-level stuttering course, and she accepted.

Throughout graduate school, I averaged about three to four hours of sleep per night and was constantly exhausted. My only hope to stay engaged in class, let alone awake, was in the hands of the instructors that made it a point to be compelling. For me, Gail was one of those professors. Early on in the course, Gail mentioned that she stutters. This was very interesting to me because I didn't hear her stuttering when she lectured. I was under the very naive impression that she had been "cured." Looking back at it now, I had a lot to learn about the true nature of stuttering.

Perhaps the aspect of this class that caught my attention most was when Gail told us stories about reactions people had to her stuttering when she was younger. So many of these stories were heartbreaking. She also showed us short clips from other documentaries that featured people who stutter, and they shared the profound emotional impact that stuttering had on their lives. I found these testimonials to be very earnest and heartfelt. At a certain point, I realized that we were no longer talking about the science of communication disorders; we were talking about the complex emotions of the human condition.

Being drawn to stuttering was no accident. Although I never stuttered, I feel that certain events in my life served as a bridge to help me relate to the lived experience of stuttering. One factor was that I was bullied as a child. To elaborate upon my experiences with bullying would be a whole other chapter.

Suffice it to say, nine out of ten kids who stutter have to contend with bullying. I know, first hand, the hell this can be in a child's life.

I had also experienced severe vocal strain for a period in my life. During that time I would withdraw from communication in social situations because I did not want to experience pain when I talked. It was disorienting because I had always spoken my mind openly and, during this time, I did not feel at liberty to do that. I do not mean to, in any way, conflate these experiences with stuttering or say that I know what it is to stutter on a personal level. I just mean to acknowledge that there was a small point of personal connection when I first heard about the negative feelings sometimes associated with stuttering.

Sitting in the back of Gail's class, absorbing and processing all of this deeply humanistic material, it first occurred to me to make a documentary about stuttering. I thought that if you could take the powerful things that people who stutter were saying and frame them with a modern production look, you would have something truly compelling. The idea excited me!

Shortly after the thought hit me, I began making grand proclamations about producing a film on stuttering one day. Sometimes having a big mouth is a detriment, but this was a rare case where it was an advantage because I had committed myself to something big! I mean . . . what could go wrong? I knew that I could operate a camera, capture sound, and edit well enough to successfully film a wedding. How much more difficult could making a documentary be? If only I knew then what I know now.

It took four years from that first moment of inspiration before I took a single step toward making the film. Truth be told, many things kept me from beginning production. Some of the factors were fear of the unknown, lack of funding, lack of experience, not being classically trained in film school, unsupportive voices in my life, and not having enough time in my schedule.

When I finally began production, it was a rush! The process was both scary and fun. It's hard to say what the best part of the process might have been because so many aspects of making a film are exciting. If I had to choose one thing, I would say that I really enjoyed being on the road and capturing the interviews themselves. Meeting all of those compelling individuals and hearing about their journeys was just golden! I was often surprised by how open many of the participants had been with some of the private and personal elements of their lives. Their vulnerability and honesty provided such rich raw material for the film. As much of a blessing as this was, it also contributed to my biggest challenge.

When someone divulges personal aspects of their life, it is precious. While I was grateful for the material I had been given, I also felt the enormous weight of responsibility to get the film done "right." Each participant sat down for an interview knowing that this film could go out to the world, and they chose to share some of their most vulnerable moments with stuttering. Issues of suicide, loneliness, hopelessness, abuse, and other such intimate topics were put into my hands as a storyteller with great trust. In the end, it was clear the interviewees had done their part, and now it was time for me to do mine. Thoughts such as "don't screw this up" began running in a loop in my mind. I wanted to do justice to these stories, and I certainly didn't want to let anyone down. This thought became paralyzing at times and weeks would go by with only incremental progress.

At a certain point, I had many disparate parts of the film that worked well as standalone pieces. However, it became difficult to see how all of them were going to come together in any kind of cohesive way to make a unified documentary. I continued to work on the film and, when I wasn't working on it, I talked about it. I discovered that simply talking about a challenge is helpful, even if you don't arrive at a solution. Luckily for me, I had many great people to talk to and, with their encouragement, I continued to move forward.

There were two "voila" moments when I knew *WHEN I STUTTER* was coming together. One was when my good friend and mentor Steve Paulson encouraged me to show what I had to some of the students at Cal State, LA. Although far from complete, this screening was extremely well received by the students, and I got a glimmer of what the film could be.

The second pivotal moment came when I showed the film to Scott Palasik for the first time. If you have seen *WHEN I STUTTER*, you will know Scott as a participant, as well as a creative contributor (on many levels). As a birthday gift from his lovely wife, he had flown to Los Angeles to view a rough cut of the film. I pressed the play bar and sat back as Scott watched the film. I knew that if it didn't cut the mustard with him, I might have to rethink the whole thing. Upon screening the 3-hour version of the film, Scott simply said, "There is nothing out there like this." He encouraged me to stay the course, and I did for the next several months. I worked and worked until the final version was completed. On April 2, 2017, after four-and-a-half years of toiling, *WHEN I STUTTER* had its world premiere to a sold-out audience at the Cleveland International Film Festival.

To date, *WHEN I STUTTER* has screened more than 125 times worldwide. These screenings have ranged from big theatrical presentations in multiplexes to smaller, community-based, screenings. The film has been an official selection for 15 film festivals and honored with seven awards. It has had the distinction of being screened at the National Stuttering Association Convention (2017), the American Speech and Hearing Association (ASHA) Convention (2017), the World Congress of Stuttering (2018), and the California Speech and Hearing (CSHA) Conference for three years in a row (2017–2019). *WHEN I STUTTER* has also been translated into nine different languages, and six more are currently in progress. Among my proudest achievements is the fact that more than 100 universities and organizations are using my film to educate their students, faculty members, and library patrons about the true nature of stuttering. It is also available as a professional development course online through XceptionalED.

My Gifts

WHEN I STUTTER has been, by far, my greatest achievement. It has, in many ways changed my life and opened up so many doors and great opportunities. I say none of this to boast but rather as a person who is still stunned and bewildered by what can come from a single idea. The film has had so many remarkable accomplishments, and not a fraction of them were expected during the making of the film, nor when it was completed. If I'm being candid, I had initially hoped that it might play at a couple of universities and maybe, just maybe, a single film festival. The direction the film has taken has been the stuff of dreams, and it has changed my life.

If I have a gift, I would have to say that it is one that I share with a fictitious boxing character from Philadelphia who came to the world's attention in 1976, Rocky Balboa. I have always loved the idea of Rocky because he represents such a gritty and heartfelt version of the American Dream. The interesting part is that he wasn't a great fighter in the classic sense. His boxing abilities were depicted as crude and underwhelming. He did have one great gift though, and that was that he could withstand more punishment than the next guy.

In his fights, Rocky would get knocked down only to get back up time after time. In one critical moment, his manager urged him to "stay down" for safety reasons, but he just got back up again. In the end, he was able to take more punches than his opponent, and he was literally the last man standing. This is where we overlap. I feel that resilience is my gift, too. Although I probably couldn't take a lot of real punches—not like Rocky anyway, I do have a high threshold for pain, disappointment, and all manner of setbacks that life can throw at you. It may be inadvisable at times, but I just keep getting back up and moving forward. It's a necessity.

My Recommendations

1. **Surround yourself with positive and honest people.** Any meaningful endeavor is going to be fraught with self-doubt, and you don't need negativity from people

further hampering your project. Having the right people around you will make all the difference—trust me. Nothing will kill a project like negativity and the constant sowing of doubt. On the other end of the spectrum, having people tell you that something is "great" when it's not is also not productive. A balance can be struck between positivity and honesty. They need to go hand-in-hand for a project to grow.

2. **Choose your medium for sharing your story.** If you are going into filmmaking, know that you have picked one of the most challenging ways to express your artistic or educational vision. While no path is ever "easy," other avenues might be more fitting. An outlet such as writing is less taxing and much less expensive and so are many other creative options. If a story can be effectively told in any other way (for example, as an article, a book, a blog, a podcast, through photography, etc.), then I'd highly recommend telling it that way. But if it MUST be conveyed through a film, just know that many challenges lie ahead, and be resilient—KEEP GOING!

3. **Set a deadline.** Set goals for yourself to present your material, even rough versions of it, at specific points in time. At least for me, deadlines can be very galvanizing for a project. While this may put some time pressure on you, it will keep you focused on a specific point in time when you will be asked to put forth something presentable. It may not be representative of your best work or even the final product, but it will keep you moving forward. Sometimes the quest for perfection can stifle a project. A less than perfect idea that has

been put into the world is far better than a perfect idea that will never be shared. I believe this to be true in education as well as art. Leonardo da Vinci is believed to have said, "Art is never finished, only abandoned." What if he had never shared his work because it wasn't perfect?

My Wish for You

As any director will tell you, setbacks can and will occur when making a film. Sometimes they are devastating. You just have to get up and keep moving forward. Successfully contending with the setbacks I faced when making *WHEN I STUTTER* has only reinforced my belief in the essential nature of resilience in an artist's life. Resilience may be one of the greatest assets we can have when taking on a big project.

My wish for you, in your creative endeavors, is to "GET UP" every time you feel knocked down. Count on setbacks because they will always be there! There will be self-doubt, naysayers, financial difficulty, lapses in judgment, a lack of confidence, a feeling of being lost, and on and on. Get up, and move forward!

My Community

Listen to my episode on the Xceptional Leaders podcast:

When I Stutter Documentaries and SLPs with John Gomez

Ways to Connect with Me

Website: www.WhenIStutter.org

Email: john@whenistutter.org

Facebook: @WhenIStutter

Instagram: @when_i_stutter

IMDB: https://www.imdb.com/title/tt7444748/

John Gomez works as a speech pathologist for the Los Angeles Unified School District and as a professor at California State University, Los Angeles. He is also a documentary filmmaker. His feature film, WHEN I STUTTER, has been in more than 15 film festivals worldwide and has won seven awards. John was honored with the Lois V. Douglass Distinguished Alumnus Award from CSULA and the Emerging Filmmaker Award from the Chagrin Documentary Film Festival.

Age Defying

Sharing, Supporting, and Shining

Cassidy Huff

Photo by Christopher Nelson

I've always known that I was meant to be a musician. Ever since I was little, I would watch people sing and perform on television, and it enthralled me. I was so mesmerized by the music and movements that seemed to effortlessly flow out of the artist. I knew I wanted to be that person up there in front of the public.

So when my mom and grandma sat me down at the age of eight and told me that being a musician wasn't realistic, I was determined to prove them wrong. I understand now, at 17 years old, that they were just trying to help prepare me for the real world. I'm glad they had this conversation with me because it was kind of a wakeup call, but I remember thinking, "You'll see when I win my first Grammy, Tony, or Oscar."

My Inspiration

Unfortunately, this wasn't the last experience I had with people doubting my ability to succeed in the music business. I've had many more people tell me that it's an "unrealistic" career, or I look too different, or I'm not talented enough. On the flip side, I have had a huge cheering section, too! My mom and grandma realized after they had that conversation with me that I feed on people telling me that I can't do something. That's the number one thing that pushes me to be better at whatever I'm doing at that moment, whether it's school, music, acting, sports, or life in general. I have even had school personnel tell me that I needed to find more realistic goals, or set my sights on different choices that were within my reach.

Again this drives me to be better, to achieve more, to show the world my talents, to share how I can positively impact people.

Throwing myself into the performing industry at the very young age of eight, I learned a lot of things the hard way. I learned that the world is evolving and changing daily. Our world is becoming more aware of the oppression that people with disabilities face every day. Yet, no one with a disability was in the performing arts industry for me to look up to. It's incredibly difficult to see a future in a career when you can't see anyone that looks like you doing what you want to do. I have performed all over the place, and rarely have I met anyone who has any sort of disability like I have.

Let me share more about my diagnosis. I was born with a very rare genetic condition called Conradi-Hünermann syndrome. I am half blind and half deaf. Plus, my entire right side (including my lung) is three-and-a-half inches shorter than my left, so I have to wear a foot-on-foot prosthetic to help me walk. I also have kyphoscoliosis, meaning my spine bends and twists, so 41 of my grand total of 43 surgeries were on my spine. I knew that no one in the entertainment and performing arts world looked like me, but to not have anyone with any disability to look up to in the industry was what drove all my determination.

I realized that I would have to help pave the way for performers in the arts to be accurately represented like everyone else. Performers with disabilities are extremely underrepresented in mass media, movies, television, and the music industry and on stage.

I want to be what I didn't have growing up. I want to inspire people all over the world who watch me perform to think, "If she can do that, maybe I can too," regardless of their disability.

Growing up, I faced a lot of bullying. I was teased for everything I did, how I looked, and how I acted. At first it was just kids my age staring and making fun of me, but it became relentless physical bullying that occurred every day.

As I got older and started putting myself out there more, the social media bullying started. In addition, as I approached and attended high school, people started saying things behind my back. While my peers constantly compete for who has the nicest car or cutest boyfriend or brag about what party they went to over the weekend, I am so far removed from that. I'm not even focused on the typical high school events. Some of the girls won't even talk to me because they are jealous of some of the things I have done, where I get to perform, who I am on stage with, and so many other reasons. Some have even told me to my face that they don't like me, so I tend to stay to myself and not share too much.

My Gifts

I'm not sure how I remained so calm and mature about the bullying when I was younger. As any young child who has been bullied, I sometimes came home in tears. But at the end of the day, I've always known that I'm not anything those bullies tell me I am. I constantly remind myself whenever I hear mean things said about me that that person is probably repeating exactly what is being said to them. This mindset has taught me to be so much more empathetic and patient with others.

As I have gained more of a following on social media, I have experienced so much more love than hate. People's constant uplifting comments and direct messages are something that I have learned to love about having a presence on social media. I have also been able to find others with my same condition. Conradi-Hünermann is extremely rare, so finding somebody who has it is a pretty big deal.

I've been direct messaged a couple of times by individuals who have my condition, and I have been able to then connect them to our Facebook support group! I once received a private message from a mom in another country who had a very young daughter who was just diagnosed with my condition. She introduced herself and her daughter, told me a little bit about their story, and ended the message with this question that broke my heart: "Can you please just tell me that my daughter will be able to lead a happy, successful, and complete life?"

At this point my heart shattered, but her question also became a driving force behind why I do what I do. I have always wanted to be a voice in the performing arts industry that advocates for the representation of artists with disabilities. But this one question drove me further into my advocacy. I have gained a lot of knowledge over the past nine years. I have been able to grow in my knowledge of the music and performing arts industry as well as in my knowledge of disability underrepresentation in both of these industries.

My musical abilities have also grown through my amazing support systems and teachers in the industry who I've had over the years. I've also grown in my self-confidence, teaching skills, and public speaking skills since I first entered this industry.

When you've been doing a job for so long, it's impossible not to grow. You can always find an area that needs growth in your life and career.

My Recommendations

Through my experiences of overcoming adversity, ongoing education, and teaching, I share these personal recommendations with you as you create and grow your disability-focused offering:

1. **Don't give up.** Some people and obstacles will always be in your way. It's your job to find out how you can overcome their negativity.
2. **Find your purpose.** Figure out what you're really trying to accomplish. Find your thing you want to tell the world and run with it.
3. **Choose one goal (at first).** Most of us have that one thing that seems absolutely impossible to get to. You can't change the world overnight. But you can come up with one small goal to complete every day to help you get there.
4. **Realize that your work is never finished.** At the end of achieving a really amazing goal of mine, I always find myself asking, "What's next?" I've come to realize more work ALWAYS needs to be done, and one more person always needs help.
5. **Notice and understand that you have a gift.** Understand that you have something you can offer the world. You can make this planet we live on a better

place. The only way to achieve those "completely unrealistic," "out of reach," and "impossible" goals is to first acknowledge that you have a gift within yourself. I want you to know that this journey that you're embarking on isn't easy. You will have to face a lot of obstacles and have to jump over a lot of hurdles to get where you want to be.

I had to learn a lot about this industry at a very young age. That's why it's my mission to help people like YOU anytime I get a chance!

Here are a couple of things I had to learn the hard way, so you don't have to:

SLOW DOWN: It seems like such an easy concept, doesn't it? But when you're working as hard as you are to make the world a better place, it can be so difficult to not overwork yourself! Figure out where your point of exhaustion is, and come up with some strategies and self-care rituals so you don't hit that point of exhaustion. I know it sounds dumb, but trust me, it works!

IT'S OKAY TO SAY "NO": This is something I have struggled with for years and continue to wrestle with every day. When you're first starting out, opportunities fly at you from every which way, and it's so hard to say "no." I'm a people pleaser, so when I say "no," I feel like I'm letting somebody down. Sometimes that is the case, but this is okay! It's okay to tell people "no" to ensure that you can care for yourself. You don't have to be busy every day of the week. Find something besides performing that you love, and make time for that every week.

Over the years, I've come up with a system. When an exciting or enticing opportunity comes my way, I stop and check in with myself. I ask, "Do I have the mental, physical, and emotional capacity to take this project on?" If the answer isn't 100% "yes," I have to say, "Thanks but no thanks," to that opportunity. Part of life is learning how to say "no" and being okay with doing so!

You can't say "yes" to everything, otherwise you'll experience burn out. And that's not a good thing for anyone

FOCUS ON SELF-CARE: Earlier, I mentioned something called "self-care." You're probably rolling your eyes at me because when people used to say it to me, I did the same thing. But self-care is one of the most important things about running a brand and/or business. If you're not okay, how can you expect your business and employees to be? It all starts with you. Even if it's something as small as taking a shower, drinking some tea, or taking some time to meditate and reflect, it needs to happen. When you're so busy running a business, you forget that YOU MATTER TOO! So please, make it a goal for yourself today to take twenty or thirty minutes to just focus on you!

My Wish for You

If you don't have anybody else to say it to you today, I'm proud of you, you're going to change the world for the better, people need you, and you matter!

One of my favorite quotes that motivates me when these obstacles get in my way is from the one and only Lin-Manuel Miranda in *Hamilton*, "I am not throwing away my shot." So you shouldn't throw yours away either.

Remember to have fun, enjoy the little moments, and above all else, be proud of yourself! You've made it this far, let's see how much farther you can make it. Go change some lives!

My Community

Listen to my episode on the Xceptional Leaders podcast:

An Exceptional Teenage Life with Cassidy Huff

Ways to Connect with Me

Website: www.cassidyhuff.com

LinkedIn: Cassidy Huff

Facebook: Cassidy Huff

Instagram: @cass_huff

Twitter: @cass_huff

Cassidy Huff is an eighteen-year-old actress and singer-songwriter from Seattle, Wash.. Cassidy has performed on stages all over the world and is looking forward to pursuing her bachelor of fine arts degree in musical theater at The American Musical and Dramatic Academy in Los Angeles, Calif., starting in the fall of 2020.

Final Thoughts

As I review final edits and write this last chapter in June 2020, the world is currently focused on an outbreak caused by the coronavirus disease 2019 (COVID-19), first identified in Wuhan City, Hubei Province, China. Entire countries have been quarantined and are slowly navigating the path to safe public interactions, Black Monday tumbled the stock market on March 9, schools all over the world were closed and moved to online learning, and people marched daily to demand change, fairness, and justice for the black community. It seems irresponsible not to include this as a point of reference for you.

The majority of the authors had already written their chapters by the time the virus reached the United States, and suddenly, I was tasked with reassessing the launch timeline for this book and postponing the public sharing of their beautiful stories. What has been more difficult is hearing how many of our clients and communities with autism and emotional disabilities are struggling with increased anxiety related to current events and knowing that so many of my personal friends with disabilities are considered immunocompromised and high risk for contracting the virus.

I have taken comfort from connecting with the authors and others in my Brilliance Zone Facebook group. This group was created to unite disability *leaders*. This means that during this time of increasing turmoil and anxiety, the majority of the members and authors are being called on to provide guidance, support, information, and resources, in addition to addressing rightful concerns regarding their own health, as well as the health of their loved ones. Through their shared stories of selfless giving, I am reminded of what it means to be an Exceptional Leader and am redirected to the overall value of this book.

Now three months later than our previously planned launch date, several authors, mentors, and friends have encouraged me to push forward and share this book as a gift of love and positivity to the world. Respecting the timing of marketing and social media posts during such a period of upheaval regarding health, finances, and daily living is something we needed to weigh heavily.

It is here where we pause to reconsider our original collective intention:

To open our hearts, share the most personal viewpoints related to our journeys, and inspire you to take action to find ways to help more people with disabilities.

Thank you for supporting us, and we hope you have enjoyed learning more about us, our motivation, and our experiences. As the majority of our voices have echoed, it doesn't take one enormous action. It is a series of smaller actions, including reading this book, that will take you on your own journey and path to becoming an Exceptional Leader.

As you have experienced, our individual contact information is included with each chapter. Reach out to us! Let us know your thoughts, tell us your experience, and join us on our journey! We would love to connect directly with YOU beyond the words in this book. Together we can do more, and we want to know how you can be a part of the giving, creating, and supporting—right alongside us.

Have your own idea you want to noodle on? We invite you to join our Facebook group to connect and share your ideas, feedback, challenges, and journey to becoming an Exceptional Leader!

The world is so much smaller these days thanks to advanced technologies. Please don't let the barriers of location keep you from envisioning, connecting, and realizing your dreams of helping more people with disabilities. We are here with you.

Becoming an Exceptional Leader

https://www.facebook.com/groups/becominganexceptionallead er